SEC 302 BAIL MATTERS- SUPREME COURT'S LEADING CASE LAWS

CASE NOTES- FACTS- FINDINGS OF APEX COURT JUDGES & CITATIONS

JAYPRAKASH BANSILAL SOMANI

Made with ♥ on the Notion Press Platform
www.notionpress.com

Dedicated

To

All the Past & Present Judges of the Supreme Court of India.

Salute to their wisdom.

Salute to their interpretation of Law.

Salute to their elaborative judgement writing.

Contents

Contents

Preface

Dear Learned Advocates of the Trial Courts, Session Courts, High Courts, Supreme Court & Individuals,

I am very delighted to provide you a book on 'Sec 302 BAIL MATTERS'-Supreme Court of India Leading Case Laws.

In this book you will get...

1. Name of the Case i. e. Cause title

2.Relevant Sections discussed in the case

3. Hon'ble Judges/Coram of the case

4.Number of PDF Pages in Original Judgement of the case

5. All available Citations of the case

6. Case Note with appeal allowed/ dismissed or disposed off

7. Facts of the case

8. Hon'ble Apex Court's findings, while dismissing/allowing or disposing the appeal

9. Ratio Decidendi if any.

My special thanks to Manupatra, because of their web portal I can compile this book in well manner. I am also thankful to Notion Press to support me to publish & market this book throughout the Country. Thanks to my Juniors, Advocate Colleagues & Insolvency Professional Colleagues to support me in this venture.

Miss Shruti Kriti has helped me a lot to compile this book.

I hope this book will add some value addition in the wealth of your legal knowledge. Your positive feedbacks will boost me to compile/ write further books & negative feedbacks will improve my skills. Kindly send your valuable feedbacks by email.

Thanks with Regards,

Jayprakash B. Somani

Advocate, Supreme Court of India

Email: jaysomani64@gmail.com

Web Site:www.jayprakashsomani.com

Call: 9322188701, 8459194576

Acknowledgements

Printed & Published by
Notion Press
No. 8, 3rd Cross Street,
CIT Colony, Mylapore,
Chennai, Tamil Nadu- 600004

ℙℙℙ

Managed by
Jayprakash Somani Advocates & Solicitors
Law Firm for Supreme Court of India
Delhi Office
B- 851, 1st Floor, Shivaji Marg, New Ashok Nagar, Delhi 110096.
Call: 9322188701, 8459194576
Supreme Court Chamber
312, 3rd Floor, M. C. Setalvad Block, In front of 'D' Gate, Bhagwan Das Road, Supreme Court of India, New Delhi 110001
Contact: 8459194576, 9811011747
www.jayprakashsomani.com

ℙℙℙ

Books are available online in India

1. Notion Press:https://notionpress.com/author/jayprakash_somani

2. Amazon:https://www.amazon.in/s?k=jayprakash+somani

3. Flipkart:https://www.flipkart.com/search?q=Jayprakash%20Somani

Books are available online at International Market

4. Amazon International: https://www.amazon.com/s?k=jayprakash+somani

5. Amazon United Kingdom: https://www.amazon.co.uk/s?k=jayprakash+somani

6. E-Books/Kindle edition at National & International Level: https://www.amazon.in/s?k=jaypraksh+somani

ℙℙℙ

ONE

PRASHANT SINGH RAJPUT VS. THE STATE OF MADHYA PRADESH AND ORS., 2021

Hon'ble Judges/Coram:Dr. D.Y. Chandrachud and B.V. Nagarathna, JJ.

Acts/ Sections: Arms Act 1959 - Section 25(1); Code of Criminal Procedure, 1973 (CrPC) - Section 154, Code of Criminal Procedure, 1973 (CrPC) - Section 161, Code of Criminal Procedure, 1973 (CrPC) - Section 164, Code of Criminal Procedure, 1973 (CrPC) - Section 173, Code of Criminal Procedure, 1973 (CrPC) - Section 438, Code of Criminal Procedure, 1973 (CrPC) - Section 439; Indian Penal Code, 1860 (IPC) - Section 34, Indian Penal Code, 1860 (IPC) - Section 294, Indian Penal Code, 1860 (IPC) - Section 302, Indian Penal Code, 1860 (IPC) - Section 323, Indian Penal Code, 1860 (IPC) - Section 324, Indian Penal Code, 1860 (IPC) - Section 379, Indian Penal Code, 1860 (IPC) - Section 506; Narcotic Drugs And Psychotropic Substances Act, 1985 - Section 8, Narcotic Drugs And Psychotropic Substances Act, 1985 - Section 20(b)

No. of pages of the Original Judgement: 011

Citation: AIR2021SC5004, MANU/SC/0828/2021

Case Note: Criminal - Anticipatory Bail - Cancellation thereof - Section 438 of the Code of Criminal Procedure, 1973 (CrPC) - Case registered under Sections 302 and 323 read with Section 34 of the Indian Penal Code 1860(IPC) - High Court vide impugned judgment granted anticipatory bail - Judgment assailed on the grounds that High Court relied on investigation report to hold that Applicant/ Accused were not present on the spot and also ignored the gravity of offence - Whether the anticipatory bail as granted liable to be set aside?

Facts: Crime case was registered on the basis of a dehati nalsi/FIR lodged by the Appellant alleging the four Accused persons due to a previous rivalry shot deceased. Appellant was allegedly hit on his head with the butt of gun, leading to an injury. High Court had allowed the application seeking anticipatory bail noting that the investigation did not reveal that he was even present at the spot of crime. The High Court observed that the veracity of such a report could not be questioned at this stage. Further, it held that even if he was present at the spot, there was no allegation against him of having fired at the deceased. Hence, the present appeal.

Hon'ble Apex Court Held, while allowing the Appeals: The offence is of a serious nature in which Vikas Singh was murdered. The FIR and the statements Under Sections 161 and 164 of the Code of Criminal Procedure indicate a specific role to Joginder Singh and Suryabhan Singh in the crime. The order granting anticipatory bail has ignored material aspects, including the nature and gravity of the offence, and the specific allegations against Joginder Singh and Suryabhan Singh. Hence, a sufficient case has been made out for cancelling the anticipatory bail granted by the High Court. Appeals allowed. The impugned judgments granting anticipatory bail set aside.

ꝐꝐꝐ

TWO

VIPAN KUMAR DHIR VS. STATE OF PUNJAB AND ORS., 2021

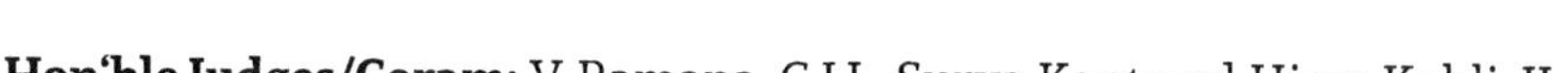

Hon'ble Judges/Coram: V. Ramana, C.J.I., Surya Kant and Hima Kohli, JJ.

Act/ Sections: Code of Criminal Procedure, 1973 (CrPC) - Section 82; Indian Penal Code, 1860 (IPC) - Section 120B, Indian Penal Code, 1860 (IPC) - Section 302, Indian Penal Code, 1860 (IPC) - Section 304B

No. of pages of the Original Judgement: 05

Citation: AIR2021SC4865, MANU/SC/0781/2021

Case Note: Criminal - Cancellation of Bail - Challenge against grant of Anticipatory Bail - Offence allegedly committed under Sections 304B, 302 read with 120B of Indian Penal Code, 1860 (IPC) - Respondent-Accused declared remained absconder for two years - Bail granted on the undertaking to join investigation and claim of parity - Whether in the given circumstances, Bail was rightly granted?

Facts: In the instant case, challenge was made against grant of anticipatory bail to R2, the mother-in-law of the deceased. FIR was lodged against 7 Accused persons, 4 of whom were members of the in laws family of the deceased including the Respondent-Accused. Accused family members were alleged of harassing and physically torturing the deceased on the pretext of dowry demands. Vide the impugned order, High Court allowed set aside the order declaring Respondent-Accused as an absconder and also granted her anticipatory bail. Reliefs were granted on the premise of joining investigation and parity.

Hon'ble Apex Court Held, while disposing the Appeal: Cancellation of bail is to be dealt on a different footing in comparison to a proceeding for grant of bail. It is necessary that 'cogent and overwhelming reasons' are present for the cancellation of bail.

In the case in hand, the High Court seems to have been primarily swayed by the fact that the Respondent-Accused was 'co- operating' with investigation. This is, however, contrary to the record as the Respondent-Accused remained absconding for more than two years after being declared a proclaimed offender. She chose to join investigation only after securing interim bail from the High Court.

Even if there was any procedural irregularity in declaring the Respondent-Accused as an absconder, that by itself was not a justifiable ground to grant pre-arrest bail in a case of grave offence save where the High Court on perusal of case-diary and other material on record is, prima facie, satisfied that it is a case of false or over-exaggerated accusation. Such being not the case here, the High Court went on a wrong premise in granting anticipatory bail to the Respondent-Accused.

The ground of parity with co-Accused equally unwarranted. The allegations in the FIR against the Respondent-Mother-in-Law and her younger son materially different.

Impugned order set aside. Appeals disposed of accordingly.

THREE

State of Haryana Vs. Ram Mehar and Ors., 2016

Hon'ble Judges/Coram: Dipak Misra and U.U. Lalit, JJ.

Act/ Sections: Indian Evidence Act, 1872 - Section 138, Indian Evidence Act, 1872 - Section 165; Code of Criminal Procedure, 1973 (CrPC) - Section 172(2), Code of Criminal Procedure, 1973 (CrPC) - Section 231(2), Code of Criminal Procedure, 1973 (CrPC) - Section 309, Code of Criminal Procedure, 1973 (CrPC) - Section 311, Code of Criminal Procedure, 1973 (CrPC) - Section 313, Code of Criminal Procedure, 1973 (CrPC) - Section 406, Code of Criminal Procedure, 1973 (CrPC) - Section 482; Code of Criminal Procedure, 1882 (CrPC) - Section 540; Indian Penal Code, 1860 (IPC) - Section 34, Indian Penal Code, 1860 (IPC) - Section 114, Indian Penal Code, 1860 (IPC) - Section 120B, Indian Penal Code, 1860 (IPC) - Section 147, Indian Penal Code, 1860 (IPC) - Section 148, Indian Penal Code, 1860 (IPC) - Section 149, Indian Penal Code, 1860 (IPC) - Section 201, Indian Penal Code, 1860 (IPC) - Section 302, Indian Penal Code, 1860 (IPC) - Section 307, Indian Penal Code, Constitution of India - Article 14, Constitution of India - Article 21, Constitution of India - Article 136

No. of pages of the Original Judgement: 20

Citation: AIR2016SC3942, AIR2016SC3942, (2016)8SCC762, MANU/SC/0938/2016

Case Note: Criminal - Application to recall witnesses - Section 311 of Code of Criminal Procedure, 1973 - Prosecution case - Accused persons being armed - Went inside Manesar Factory of Maruti Suzuki Limited - Smashed glass walls of the conference room - Threw chairs and table tops - Towards management officials - Surrounded conference hall from all sides - Gave threats - Doing away with lives of officials present there - Exhortation continued for quite a length of time - Attempts made to burn alive the officials - Entire office set on fire - Efforts by officials to escape - Futile - Accused persons blocked the staircases - Police officials who arrived at the spot - Assaulted - Obstructed from saving the officials - Officials were saved by police - Fire brought under control - However, General Manager, Human Resources - Burnt alive - FIR lodged - After completion of investigation - Police filed chargesheet - Against 148 workers - Various offences - Matter committed to Court of Session - Evidence of the prosecution - Recording of statements of accused persons Under Section 313 Code of Criminal Procedure - Concluded - After statement under Section 313 Code of Criminal Procedure recorded - Defence also adduced its evidence - Examined witnesses - Application for bail filed before trial Court - Rejected upto High Court - Some accused persons moved this Court - Court did not pass any order on bail application - Directed learned Sessions Judge - Dispose trial expeditiously - Two petitions under Section 311 - Code of Criminal Procedure - Filed by different accused persons - Recall of certain witnesses - Trial Court observed - Application moved at very belated stage -102 prosecution witnesses were already examined - Court noted - Long time was consumed for recording statements - More than last six months - Case being adjourned - Recalled direction of this Court - Try the matter expeditiously - Trial Court held - When material questions - Already been put - No point to entertain application - Mere change of counsel - Not be considered a ground - Allow the application - Dissatisfied, accused persons preferred CRM-Ms - Section 482 of Code of Criminal Procedure - High Court took note of common ground - Leading counsel for defence - Critically ill during trial - Due to inadvertence - Certain important questions, suggestions and allegations, etc. - Not put to said witnesses - Senior lawyer engaged at final stage - Such inadvertent errors discovered by him - Needed to be rectified - Have a meaningful defence - Fair trial - High Court held - Case for recalling had been made out - Allowed the petitions - Set aside the order of Trial Court - Present appeal against order of High Court - Whether the order of the High Court allowing the application is sustainable in law - Whether the reasons ascribed by the High Court are germane for exercise of power Under Section 311 Code of Criminal Procedure

Facts: The prosecution case before the trial court is that the accused persons being armed went inside M1 room of the Manesar Factory of Maruti Suzuki Limited, smashed the glass walls of the conference room and threw chairs and table tops towards the management officials, surrounded the conference hall from all sides and gave threats of doing away with the lives of the officials present over there. The exhortation continued for quite a length of time. All kind of attempts were made to burn alive the officials of the management. During this pandemonium, the entire office was set on fire by the accused persons and the effort by the officials to escape became an exercise in futility as the accused persons had blocked the staircases. The police officials who arrived at the spot were assaulted by the workers and they were obstructed from going upstairs to save the officials. Despite the obstruction, the officials were saved by the police and the fire was brought under control by the fire brigade.

In the incident where chaos was the sovereign, Mr. Avnish Dev, General Manager, Human Resources of the Company was burnt alive. The said occurrence led to lodging of FIR at Police Station Manesar. After completion of the investigation, the police filed charge sheet against 148 workers in respect of various offences before the competent court which, in turn, committed the matter to the court of session and during trial the accused persons were charged for the offences punishable Under

Sections147/148/149/452/302/307/436/323/332/353/427/114/201/120B/34/325/381 & 382 Indian Penal Code.

The evidence of the prosecution and recording of statements of accused persons Under Section 313 Code of Criminal Procedure was concluded. After the statement Under Section 313 Code of Criminal Procedure were recorded, defence also adduced its evidence by examining 15 witnesses. When an application for bail was filed before the trial court and it was rejected upto High Court, some accused persons moved this Court by filing Special Leave Petition (Criminal) wherein the Court did not pass any order on the bail application. The Court directed the learned Session Judge to dispose of the trial as expeditiously as possible.

When the matter stood thus, two petitions Under Section 311 of Code of Criminal Procedure were filed by different accused persons for recall of certain witnesses.

The Trial Court observed that the application was moved at a very belated stage at a time when 102 prosecution witnesses were already examined during the trial in which larger number of 148 accused are involved. The Court also noted that long time was consumed for recording the statements of the accused Under Section 313 Code of Criminal Procedure and for more than the last six months, the case was being adjourned for recording the defence evidence. The Court also recalled the direction of this Court to decide the trial expeditiously.

The Trial Court, thus, came to hold that when the material questions had already been put, there was no point to entertain the application and mere change of the counsel could not be considered as a ground to allow the application for recalling the witnesses for the purpose of further cross-examination.

Dissatisfied with aforesaid orders, the accused persons preferred CRM-Ms before the High Court Under Section 482 Code of Criminal Procedure. The High Court took note of the common ground that the leading counsel for the defence was critically ill during the trial and due to inadvertence, certain important questions, suggestions with respect to the individual roles and allegations against the respective accused persons, the injuries sustained by the witnesses, as well as the alleged weapons of offence used, had not been put to the said witnesses. It also took note of the fact that the senior lawyer had been engaged at the final stage and such inadvertent errors were discovered by him and they needed to be rectified in order to have a meaningful defence and a fair trial. The High Court came to hold that a case for recalling had been made out to ensure grant of fair opportunity to defend and uphold the concept of fair trial. The High Court, thus, allowed the petitions and set aside the order of the Trial Court. Hence, the present appeal against the order of the High Court.

Hon'ble Apex Court Held, while allowing the appeals: Before the Court adverted to the ambit and scope of Section 311 Code of Criminal Procedure and its attract ability to the existing factual matrix, it was thought imperative to dwell upon the concept of "fair trial". There is no denial of the fact that fair trial is an in segregable facet of Article 21 of the Constitution. This Court on numerous occasions has emphasized on the fundamental conception of fair trial as the majesty of law so commands.

The various decisions of this Court when analysed appositely clearly convey that the concept of the fair trial is not in the realm of abstraction. It is not a vague idea. It is a concrete phenomenon. It is not rigid and there cannot be any strait-jacket formula for applying the same. On occasions it has the necessary flexibility. Therefore, it cannot be attributed or clothed with any kind of rigidity or flexibility in its application. It is because fair trial in its ambit requires fairness to the accused, the victim and the collective at large. Neither the accused nor the prosecution nor the victim which is a part of the society can claim absolute predominance over the other. Once absolute predominance is recognized, it will have the effect potentiality to bring in an anarchical disorder in the conducting of trial defying established legal norm. There should be passion for doing justice but it must be commanded by reasons and not propelled by any kind of vague instigation. It would be dependent on the fact situation; established norms and recognized principles and eventual appreciation of the factual scenario in entirety.

There may be cases which may command compartmentalization but it cannot be stated to be an inflexible rule. Each and every irregularity cannot be imported to the arena of fair trial. There may be situations where injustice to the victim may play a pivotal role. The centripodal purpose is to see that injustice is avoided when the trial is conducted. Simultaneously the concept of fair trial cannot be allowed to such an extent so that the systemic order of conducting a trial in accordance with Code of Criminal Procedure or other enactments get mortgaged to the whims and fancies of the defence or the prosecution. The command of the Code cannot be thrown to winds. In such situation, as has been laid down in many an authority, the courts have significantly an eminent role.

A plea of fairness cannot be utilized to build Castles in Spain or permitted to perceive a bright moon in a sunny afternoon. It cannot be acquiesced to create an organic disorder in the system. It cannot be acceded to manure a fertile mind to usher in the nemesis of the concept of trial as such. From the aforesaid it may not be understood that it has been impliedly stated that the fair trial should not be kept on its own pedestal. It ought to remain in its desired height but as far as its applicability is concerned, the party invoking it has to establish with the support of established principles. Be it stated when the process of the court is abused in the name of fair trial at the drop of a hat, there is miscarriage of justice. And, justice, the queen of all virtues, sheds tears. That is not unthinkable and the Court had no hesitation in saying so.

Having dwelled upon the concept of fair trial, the Court proceeded to the principles laid down in precedents of this Court, applicability of the same to a fact situation and duty of the court Under Section 311 Code of Criminal Procedure.

Keeping in mind the principles stated in the authorities referred to by the Court, the defensibility of the order passed by the High Court had to be tested. The Court has already reproduced the assertions made in the petition seeking recall of witnesses. It has, for obvious reasons, also reproduced certain passages from the trial court judgment. The grounds urged before the trial court fundamentally pertain to illness of the counsel who was engaged on behalf of the defence and his inability to put questions with regard to weapons mentioned in the FIR and the weapons that are referred to in the evidence of the witnesses. That apart, it has been urged that certain suggestions could not be given. The marrow of the grounds relates to the illness of the counsel. It needs to be stated that the learned trial Judge who had the occasion to observe the conduct of the witnesses and the proceedings in the trial, has clearly held that recalling of the witnesses were not necessary for just decision of the case.

The High Court, as the Court noticed, had referred to certain authorities and distinguished the decision in State (NCT of Delhi) v. Shiv Kumar Yadav and Anr. and U.T. of Dadra and Nagar Haveli and Anr. v. Fatehsinh Mohansinh Chauhan. The High Court has opined that the court has to be magnanimous in permitting mistakes to be rectified, more so, when the prosecution was permitted to lead additional evidences by invoking the provisions Under Section311 Code of Criminal Procedure. The High Court has also noticed that the accused persons are in prison and, therefore, it should be justified to allow the recall of witnesses.

The heart of the matter is whether the reasons ascribed by the High Court are germane for exercise of power Under Section 311 Code of Criminal Procedure. The criminal trial is required to proceed in accordance with Section 309 of the Code of Criminal Procedure.

There is a definite purpose in referring to the authorities. The Court is absolutely conscious about the factual matrix in the said cases. The observations were made in the context where examination-in-chief was deferred for quite a long time and the procrastination ruled as the Monarch. Court's reference to the said authorities should not be construed to mean that Section 311 Code of Criminal Procedure should not be allowed to have its full play. But, a prominent one, the courts cannot ignore the factual score. Recalling of witnesses as envisaged under the said statutory provision on the grounds that accused persons are in custody, the prosecution was allowed to recall some of its witnesses earlier, the counsel was ill and magnanimity commands fairness should be shown, the Court was inclined to think, are not acceptable in the obtaining factual matrix.

The decisions which have used the words that the court should be magnanimous, needless to give special emphasis, did not mean to convey individual generosity or magnanimity which is founded on any kind of fanciful notion. It has to be applied on the basis of judicially established and accepted principles. The approach may be liberal but that does not necessarily mean "the liberal approach" shall be the Rule and all other parameters shall become exceptions. Recall of some witnesses by the prosecution at one point of time, can never be ground to entertain a petition by the defence though no acceptable ground is made out. It is not an arithmetical distribution. This kind of reasoning can be dangerous. In the case at hand, the prosecution had examined all the witnesses. The statements of all the accused persons, that is 148 in number, had been recorded Under Section 313 Code of Criminal Procedure. The defence had examined 15 witnesses. The foundation for recall, as is evincible from the applications filed, does not even remotely make out a case that such recalling is necessary for just decision of the case or to arrive at the truth.

The singular ground which prominently comes to surface is that the earlier counsel who was engaged by the defence had not put some questions and failed to put some questions and give certain suggestions. It has come on record that number of lawyers were engaged by the defence. The accused persons had engaged counsel of their choice. In such a situation recalling of witnesses indubitably cannot form the foundation. If it is accepted as a ground, there would be possibility of a retrial. There may be an occasion when such a ground may weigh with the court, but definitely the instant case does not arouse the judicial conscience within the established norms of Section 311 Code of Criminal Procedure for exercise of such jurisdiction. It is noticeable that the High Court has been persuaded by the submission that recalling of witnesses and their cross-examination would not take much time and that apart, the cross-examination could be restricted to certain aspects. In this regard, the Court was obliged to observe that the High Court has failed to appreciate that the witnesses have been sought to be recalled for further cross-examination to elicit certain facts for establishing certain discrepancies; and also, to be given certain suggestions. The Court was disposed to think that this kind of plea in a case of this nature and at this stage could not have been allowed to be entertained.

At this juncture, the Court thought it apt to state that the exercise of power Under Section 311 Code of Criminal Procedure can be sought to be invoked either by the prosecution or by the accused persons or by the Court itself. The High Court has been moved by the ground that the accused persons are in the custody and the concept of speedy trial is not nullified and no prejudice is caused, and, therefore, the principle of magnanimity should apply. Suffice it to say, a criminal trial does not singularly centre around the accused. In it there is involvement of the prosecution, the victim and the victim represent the collective. The cry of the collective may not be uttered in decibels which is physically audible in the court premises, but the Court has to remain sensitive to such silent cries and the agonies, for the society seeks justice. Therefore, a balance has to be struck. The Court had already explained the use of the words "magnanimous approach" and how it should be understood. Regard being had to the concept of balance, and weighing the factual score on the scale of balance, the Court was of the convinced opinion that the High Court has fallen into absolute error in axing the order passed by the learned trial Judge. The Court observed "If we allow ourselves to say, when the concept of fair trial is limitlessly stretched, having no boundaries, the orders like the present one may fall in the arena of sanctuary of errors." Hence, the Court reiterated the necessity of doctrine of balance.

In view of the proceeded analysis the Court allowed the appeals, set aside the order passed by the High Court and restored that of the learned trial Judge. The Court directed the learned trial judge to proceed with the trial in accordance with the law.

FOUR

Somesh Chaurasia Vs. Respondent: State of M.P. and Ors.,2021

Hon'ble Judges/Coram: Dr. D.Y. Chandrachud and Hrishikesh Roy, JJ.

Act/ Sections: Code of Criminal Procedure, 1898 (CrPC) - Section 426(1), Code of Criminal Procedure, 1898 (CrPC) - Section 426(2), Code of Criminal Procedure, 1898 (CrPC) - Section 561A; Code of Criminal Procedure, 1973 (CrPC) - Section 82, Code of Criminal Procedure, 1973 (CrPC) - Section 173(8), Code of Criminal Procedure, 1973 (CrPC) - Section 319, Code of Criminal Procedure, 1973 (CrPC) - Section 389, Code of Criminal Procedure, 1973 (CrPC) - Section 389(1), Code of Criminal Procedure, 1973 (CrPC) - Section 439, Code of Criminal Procedure, 1973 (CrPC) - Section 439(2); Constitution of India - Article 50; Indian Penal Code, 1860 (IPC) - Section 34, Indian Penal Code, 1860 (IPC) - Section 120, Indian Penal Code, 1860 (IPC) - Section 147, Indian Penal Code, 1860 (IPC) - Section 148, Indian Penal Code, 1860 (IPC) - Section 149, Indian Penal Code, 1860 (IPC) - Section 294, Indian Penal Code, 1860 (IPC) - Section 295, Indian Penal Code, 1860 (IPC) - Section 302, Indian Penal Code, 1860 (IPC) - Section 307, Indian Penal Code, 1860 (IPC) - Section 323, Indian Penal Code, 1860 (IPC) - Section 324, Indian Penal Code, 1860 (IPC) - Section 341

No. of pages of the Original Judgement: 015

Citation: AIR2021SC3563, MANU/SC/0466/2021

Case Note: Criminal - Suspension of Sentence - Revocation of order in connection related thereto - Cancellation of Bail - R2 convicted under Section 302 of the Indian Penal Code, 1860 (IPC) - High Court vide impugned judgment declined to entertain applications seeking revocation of suspension of sentence and bail granted to R2 -Whether High Court erred in declining reliefs to Appellant and sought in the backdrop of facts and circumstances?

Facts: In the instant matter High Court suspended sentence awarded during the pendency of appeal. State and Appellant sought revocation of order and also sought cancellation of bail granted to R2. Cancellation of bail was sought by Appellant on the ground that after the sentence was suspended, FIR was registered against the R2 wherein he was implicated in the murder of the Appellant's father. The State sought cancellation of bail on the ground that R2 has two other convictions against him on a charge of murder and other crime under Sections 399 and 402 of the Indian Penal Code and Section 25(1)(B)(a) of the Arms Act. Both the applications were dismissed.

Hon'ble Apex Court Held, while allowing the Appeal: The High Court misapplied itself to the legal principles which must govern such a case. The serious error by the High Court in its impugned order can be considered from two perspectives. First, the High Court by simply disposing of the IAs seeking cancellation of bail ignored material considerations which ought to have weighed in the decision. Taking the position as it stood when the High Court considered the issue, a clear case for cancellation of bail was established. The second aspect which is also of significance is the impact of the order of the High Court. The High Court was apprised of the fact that FIR No. 143 of 2019 had been lodged against the second Respondent. The investigation into the FIR had to proceed according to law. Instead, the High Court gave a period of ninety days to the police to enquire into the complaint of the second Respondent that he was being targeted and allowed the police to thereafter proceed in accordance with law. This order had the effect of obstructing a fair investigation into the FIR at the behest of the Accused despite the nature and gravity of the allegations against him. Unfortunately, the High Court failed in its duty to ensure that the sanctity of the criminal justice process is preserved. This Court has had to step in to ensure that the Rule of law is preserved.

Order of the High Court set aside. The bail granted to the second Respondent shall stand cancelled.

♡♡♡

FIVE

Kumer Singh Vs. State of Rajasthan and Ors., 2021

Hon'ble Judges/Coram: Dr. D.Y. Chandrachud and M.R. Shah, JJ.

Act/ Sections: Code of Criminal Procedure, 1973 (CrPC) - Section 161, Code of Criminal Procedure, 1973 (CrPC) - Section 439; Indian Penal Code, 1860 (IPC) - Section 147, Indian Penal Code, 1860 (IPC) - Section 148, Indian Penal Code, 1860 (IPC) - Section 149, Indian Penal Code, 1860 (IPC) - Section 302, Indian Penal Code, 1860 (IPC) - Section 307, Indian Penal Code, 1860 (IPC) - Section 323, Indian Penal Code, 1860 (IPC) - Section 341, Indian Penal Code, 1860 (IPC) - Section 427

No. of pages of the Original Judgement: 013

Citation: MANU/SC/0483/2021

Case Note: Criminal - Bail - Section 439 of the Code of Criminal Procedure, 1973 - FIR registered under Sections 147, 148, 302, 307, 323, 341, 427 read with Section 149 of the Indian Penal Code, 1860 (IPC) - High Court vide impugned judgment set aside Trial Court order rejecting Bail Applications of Accused - Hence, the present appeal -Whether bail granted to Accused liable to be set aside considering gravity and nature of offence?

Facts: Appellant lodged an FIR against the Accused for the offences under Sections 147, 148, 341, 323, 307, 427, 302 read with Section 149 of the Indian Penal Code. Accused was alleged of brutally killing Appellant's brother who was the member of the Border Security Force and was on leave. Incident resulted as a result of an altercation due to the old enmity. Charge sheets filed. Sessions judge however dismissed the bail applications. High Court vide impugned judgment enlarged accused person on bail. Hence, the present appeals.

Hon'ble Apex Court Held, while allowing the Appeals: Impugned orders passed by the High Court releasing the Accused on bail cannot be sustained. Except narrating the submissions made by Learned Counsel appearing on behalf of the Accused and the public prosecutor and the complainant there is no independent application of mind by the High Court and as such no reasons whatsoever have been assigned by the High Court releasing the Accused on bail, that too in a case where the Accused are facing the charges for the offences punishable under Sections 302 and 307 read with Section 149 of the Indian Penal Code and the other offences.

The High Court has not at all taken into consideration the facts of the case; the nature of allegations; gravity of offences and role attributed to the Accused. As a matter of fact, there is no discussion or analysis of circumstances at all.

The impugned order passed by the High Court can be said to be perverse and suffers from non-application of mind to the relevant factors to be considered while grant of bail and therefore the interference of this Court is warranted.

Impugned orders passed by the High Court granting bail to the Respondents-Accused do not pass the test laid down by this Court on grant of bail. Therefore, the impugned orders deserve to be quashed and set aside.

ppp

SIX

Shakuntala Shukla Vs. Respondent: State of Uttar Pradesh and Ors., 2021

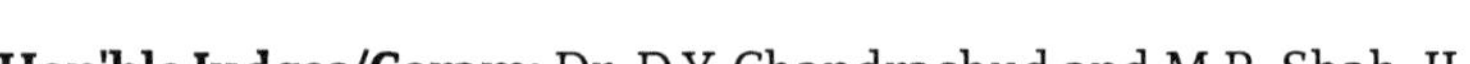

Hon'ble Judges/Coram: Dr. D.Y. Chandrachud and M.R. Shah, JJ.

Act/ Sections: Code of Criminal Procedure, 1973 (CrPC) - Section 389; Indian Penal Code, 1860 (IPC) - Section 120B, Indian Penal Code, 1860 (IPC) - Section 143, Indian Penal Code, 1860 (IPC) - Section 147, Indian Penal Code, 1860 (IPC) - Section 149, Indian Penal Code, 1860 (IPC) - Section 201, Indian Penal Code, 1860 (IPC) - Section 218, Indian Penal Code, 1860 (IPC) - Section 302, Indian Penal Code, 1860 (IPC) - Section 504, Indian Penal Code, 1860 (IPC) - Section 506

No. of pages of the Original Judgement: 08

Citation: AIR2021SC4384, MANU/SC/0611/2021

Case Note: Criminal - Enlargement on Bail - Challenge against thereto - Respondents/ Accused convicted under Sections 120B, 149, 201 and 302of the Indian Penal Code, 1860 (IPC) - Bail sought in appeals preferred allowed by the High Court - Hence the present appeal against order directing Bail - Whether High Court ought not to have allowed the bail in the instant appeal?

Facts: In the instant matter dead body of the deceased was found lying in the well. Investigation was conducted and the private Respondents Herein-Accused were convicted. Police personnel who conducted investigation was also convicted for giving false report to save accused person. In the appeal preferred against conviction, High Court vide impugned order granted bail. Hence, the present appeal.

Hon'ble Apex Court Held, while allowing the Appeal: Order granting bail to the Accused pending appeal lacks total clarity on which part of the judgment and order can be said to be submissions and which part can be said to be the findings/reasoning. It does not even reflect the submissions on behalf of the Public Prosecutor opposing the bail pending appeal.

It is not adequate that a decision is accurate, it must also be reasonable, logical, and easily comprehensible. The judicial opinion is to be written in such a way that it elucidates in a convincing manner and proves the fact that the verdict is righteous and judicious. What the court says, and how it says it, is equally important as what the court decides.

There is a total lack of clarity on the submissions, which part of the order is submission, which part of the order is the finding and/or reasoning.

Even on merits also, the impugned order passed by the High Court releasing the Accused on bail pending appeal is unsustainable. The High Court has not at all appreciated and considered the fact that the learned trial Court on appreciation of evidence has convicted the Accused for the offences under Sections 302/149, 201 r/w 120B Indian Penal Code. Once the Accused have been convicted by the learned trial Court, there shall not be any presumption of innocence thereafter. Therefore, the High Court shall be very slow in granting bail to the Accused pending appeal who are convicted for the serious offences punishable under Sections 302/149, 201 r/w 120B Indian Penal Code.

The present appeals are allowed.

ppp

SEVEN

Deep Narayan Chourasia Vs. State of Bihar, 2019

Hon'ble Judges/Coram: Abhay Manohar Sapre and Dinesh Maheshwari, JJ.

Act/ Sections: Indian Penal Code, 1860 (IPC) - Section 302; Indian Penal Code, 1860 (IPC) - Section 149; MAHARASHTRA REGIONAL AND TOWN PLANNING ACT, 1966 - Section 27

No. of pages of the Original Judgement: 07

Citation: AIR2019SC1148, (2019)13SCC153, MANU/SC/0268/2019

Case Note: Criminal - Conviction - Sections 302/149 of Indian Penal Code, 1860 (IPC); Section 27 of Arms Act - Whether High Court was right in dismissing the appeal filed by Appellant - Whether present Court should set aside entire impugned order or set aside only qua sole Appellant because other four Accused though suffered conviction under Section 302/149 of IPC alike the Appellant herein did not file any appeal against their conviction.

Facts: Five persons were tried for commission of offence of murder under Section 302/149 of IPC, 1860 (IPC) and Section 27 of Arms Act by Additional Sessions Judge. By judgment, Additional Sessions Judge convicted Accused-Kanhai Prasad Chourasia for commission of offence under Section 302 of IPC and Section 27 of Arms Act. So far as co-accused-Lukho Prasad Chourasia, Birendra Prasad Chourasia, Binod Prasad Chourasia and Deep Narayan Chourasia were concerned, all four were acquitted from charge of commission of offence under Section 302 of IPC. However, all four Accused were convicted for commission of offence under Section 27 of Arms Act and accordingly sentenced to undergo rigorous imprisonment for five years. All five Accused felt aggrieved by their respective conviction and award of jail sentence and filed two criminal appeals in High Court. High Court, however, was completely under misconception and misdirected itself by forming an opinion as if all five Accused were convicted under Section 302/149 of IPC and accordingly went on to appreciate evidence and while dismissing both appeals by a common judgment convicted four Accused under Section 302/149 of IPC along with Kanhai Prasad Chourasia. Effect of judgment of High Court was three-fold. First, both criminal appeals stand dismissed; Second, conviction and sentence of Kanhai Prasad Chourasia under Section 302 Indian Penal Code read with Section 27 of Arms Act was upheld; and third, remaining four Accused also stand convicted under Section 302 of IPC read with Section 149 of IPC and Section 27 of Arms Act. It was against this judgment, only one Accused-Deep Narayan Chourasia had felt aggrieved and filed present appeal.

Hon'ble Apex Court Held, while allowing the appeal 1. Division Bench failed to apply its judicial mind and committed fundamental jurisdictional errors.

2. First error was that, High Court proceeded on wrong factual premise that, all five Accused had suffered conviction under Section 302/149 of IPC read with Section 27 of Arms Act by Additional Sessions Judge. It was not so.

3. Second error was that, Appellant (Deep Narayan Chourasia) along with other three Accused (Lukho Prasad Chourasia, Birendra Prasad Chourasia and Binod Prasad Chourasia) were acquitted from charge of commission of offence under Section 302/149 of IPC by Additional Sessions Judge but were convicted only under Section 27 of Arms Act and were sentenced to undergo rigorous imprisonment for five years. However, as a result of High Court's order, they were convicted under Section 302/149 of Indian Penal Code without there being any appeal filed by State against order of their acquittal and without there being any notice of enhancement of their sentence issued by High Court suo motu to these four Accused.

4. Third error was that, High Court failed to see that, Additional Sessions Judge had acquitted all Accused under Section 149 of IPC, yet High Court proceeded to convict all the Accused under Section 149 of IPC without there being any appeal filed by State on this issue.

5. Fourth error was that, though High Court wrongly convicted Appellant along with three others for offence punishable under Section 302/149 of IPC, yet did not award any sentence to any of four Accused under Section 302/

149 of IPC.

6. Since, Appellant and other three Accused were acquitted of charge under Section 302/149 of IPC by Additional Sessions Judge, yet High Court convicted them under Section 302/149 of IPC for first time, sentence prescribed under Section 302/149 of IPC was mandatorily required to be awarded to each convicted Accused as provided under Section 354(3) of Code of Criminal Procedure, 1973.

7. Effect of impugned judgment, therefore, was that though Appellant along with three Accused had suffered conviction under Section 302/149 of IPC but without sentence.

8. An order, which is based entirely on wrong factual premise once held illegal by a superior Court at the instance of one Accused, cannot be allowed to stand against other non-appealing Accused persons also.

9. An illegality committed by a Court could not be allowed to be perpetuated against a person to a Lis merely because he did not bring such illegality to notice of Court and instead other person similarly placed in Lis brought such illegality to Court's notice and succeed in his challenge.

10. It would be a travesty of justice delivery system where an Accused, who was convicted of a lesser offence (Section 27 of Arms Act alone) and was acquitted of a graver offence (Section 302/149 of Indian Penal Code) was made to suffer conviction for commission of a graver offence (Section 302/149 of Indian Penal Code) without affording him of any opportunity to defend such charge at any stage of appellate proceedings.

11. If other four Accused had filed appeals in this Court, they too would have got benefit of this order. A fortiori, merely because they did not file appeals and case was now remanded for re-hearing of appeal at instance of one Accused, benefit of re-hearing of appeal could not be denied to other co-accused. Non-appealing co-accused were also entitled to get benefit of order of this Court and were, therefore, entitled for re-hearing of their appeals along with present Appellant.

12. Impugned order was set aside also qua all the Accused persons.

13. Impugned order was set aside in its entirety. Both Criminal Appeals, were restored to their original numbers before High Court for their analogues hearing.

14. Since, Appellant-Deep Narayan Chourasia out of his total jail sentence of five years awarded by Additional Sessions Judge for commission of offence under Section 27 of Arms Act had already undergone jail sentence of five months, he was released on bail to satisfaction of concerned trial Court

pending Criminal Appeals before High Court.

❦❦❦

EIGHT

NEERU YADAV VS. STATE OF U.P. AND ORS., 2015

Hon'ble Judges/Coram: Dipak Misra and Prafulla C. Pant, JJ.

Act/ Sections: Arms Act 1959 - Section 25, Arms Act 1959 - Section 27; Gangster Act - Section 2, Gangster Act - Section 3, Gangster Act - Section 60; Indian Penal Code, 1860 (IPC) - Section 34, Indian Penal Code, 1860 (IPC) - Section 120B, Indian Penal Code, 1860 (IPC) - Section 147, Indian Penal Code, 1860 (IPC) - Section 148, Indian Penal Code, 1860 (IPC) - Section 149, Indian Penal Code, 1860 (IPC) - Section 201, Indian Penal Code, 1860 (IPC) - Section 302, Indian Penal Code, 1860 (IPC) - Section 307, Indian Penal Code, 1860 (IPC) - Section 364, Indian Penal Code, 1860 (IPC) - Section 392, Indian Penal Code, 1860 (IPC) - Section 394, Indian Penal Code, 1860 (IPC) - Section 398, Indian Penal Code, 1860 (IPC) - Section 401, Indian Penal Code, 1860 (IPC) - Section 411, Indian Penal Code, 1860 (IPC) - Section 454, Indian Penal Code, 1860 (IPC) - Section 506; Code of Criminal Procedure, 1973 (CrPC) - Section 439

No. of pages of the Original Judgement: 08

Citation: AIR2015SC3703, (2016)15SCC422, MANU/SC/1086/2015

Case Note: Criminal - Legality of grant of Bail - FIR against certain persons - Chargesheet filed - Offences under Sections 147, 148, 149, 302, 307, 394, 411, 454, 506, 120B read with Section 34 Indian Penal Code, 1860 - Application for Bail - Rejected by Learned Trial Judge - Respondent No. 2 - Moved High Court - Criminal Misc. Bail Application - High Court Held - Fit case for Bail - Ground of parity - No opinion expressed on merit - High Court order under assail - Appeal by special leave - Whether in the circumstances of the case, the High Court should have enlarged Respondent No. 2 on bail on the foundation of parity

Facts: One Salek Chand s/o. Satpal Singh lodged an FIR against certain persons relating to the murder of his elder brother. Based on the lodging of the FIR, the criminal law was set in motion and eventually chargesheet was filed for the offences punishable Under Sections 147, 148, 149, 302, 307, 394, 411, 454, 506, 120B read with Section 34 Indian Penal Code, 1860. After the application for bail was rejected by the learned trial Judge, the accused person, Respondent No. 2, moved the High Court in Criminal Misc. Bail Application. It was contended that prayer for bail in respect of 11 accused persons had already been allowed, and there was no justification to deny him the said benefit as he was similarly placed. The High Court, without expressing any opinion on merit held it to be a fit case for bail. The said order is the subject matter of assail in the present appeal by special leave.

Hon'ble Apex Court Held, while allowing the appeal: (I) At the outset we are obliged to clarify that it is not an appeal seeking cancellation of bail in the strictest sense. It actually calls in question the legal pregnability of the order passed by the High Court. The prayer for cancellation of bail is not sought on the foundation of any kind of supervening circumstances or breach of any condition imposed by the High Court. The basic assail is to the manner in which the High Court has exercised its jurisdiction Under Section 439 Code of Criminal Procedure, 1973 while admitting the accused to bail. To clarify, if it has failed to take into consideration the relevant material factors, it would make the order absolutely perverse and totally indefensible. That is why there is a difference between cancellation of an order of bail and legal sustainability of an order granting bail.

(II) It is interesting to note that learned Counsel for the Appellant and the learned Counsel for the State submitted that Respondent No. 2 is still in jail despite the order of bail as he is involved in so many cases. It is submitted by learned Counsel for the Appellant that despite the factum of criminal history pointed out before the High Court, it has given it a glorious ignore which the law does not countenance. The solitary and the singular grievance which is propounded with solidity is that the High Court should have dwelt upon the same and thereafter decided the matter. In the additional affidavit, an independent chart has been filed by the State and we find that apart from the present case, there are seven cases pending against the Respondent No. 2.

(III) On a perusal of the aforesaid list, it is quite vivid that the Respondent No. 2 is a history-sheeter and is involved in heinous offences. Having stated the facts and noting the nature of involvement of the accused in the crimes in question, there can be no scintilla of doubt to name him a "history-sheeter". The question, therefore, arises whether in these circumstances, should the High Court have enlarged him on bail on the foundation of parity.

(IV) In Ram Govind Upadhyay v. Sudarshan Singh it has been clearly laid down that the grant of bail though involves exercise of discretionary power of the Court, such exercise of discretion has to be made in a judicious manner and not as a matter of course. The heinous nature of crimes warrants more caution as there is a greater chance of rejection of bail though, however, dependent on the factual matrix of the matter. It is a well settled principle of law that while dealing with an application for grant of bail, it is the duty of the Court to take into consideration certain factors and they basically are, (i) the nature of accusation and the severity of punishment in cases of conviction and the nature of supporting evidence, (ii) reasonable apprehension of tampering with the witnesses for apprehension of threat to the complainant, and (iii) Prima facie satisfaction of the court in support of the charge.

(V) We will be failing in our duty if we do not take note of the concept of liberty and its curtailment by law. It is an established fact that a crime though committed against an individual, in all cases it does not retain an individual character. It, on occasions and in certain offences, accentuates and causes harm to the society. The victim may be an individual, but in the ultimate eventuate, it is the society which is the victim. A crime, as is understood, creates a dent in the law-and-order situation. In a civilized society, a crime disturbs orderliness. It affects the peaceful life of the society. An individual can enjoy his liberty which is definitely of paramount value but he cannot be a law unto himself. He cannot cause harm to others. He cannot be a nuisance to the collective. He cannot be a terror to the society.

(VI) It is clear as cloudless sky that the High Court has totally ignored the criminal antecedents of the accused. What has weighed with the High Court is the doctrine of parity. A history-sheeter involved in the nature of crimes which we have reproduced hereinabove, are not minor offences so that he is not to be retained in custody, but the crimes are of heinous nature and such crimes, by no stretch of imagination, can be regarded as jejune.

Such cases do create a thunder and lightning having the effect potentiality of torrential rain in an analytical mind. The law expects the judiciary to be alert while admitting this kind of accused persons to be at large and, therefore, the emphasis is on exercise of discretion judiciously and not in a whimsical manner.

(VII) Before parting with the case, we may repeat with profit that it is not an appeal for cancellation of bail as the cancellation is not sought because of supervening circumstances. The annulment of the order passed by the High Court is sought as many relevant factors have not been taken into consideration which includes the criminal antecedents of the accused and that makes the order a deviant one. Therefore, the inevitable result is the lancination of the impugned order. Resultantly, the appeal is allowed and the order passed by the High Court is set aside.

NINE

BIKRAMJIT SINGH VS. THE STATE OF PUNJAB, 2020

Hon'ble Judges/Coram: Rohinton Fali Nariman, Navin Sinha and K.M. Joseph, JJ.

Act/ Sections: Arms Act, 1959 - Section 59; Code of Criminal Procedure, 1973 (CrPC) - Section 6, Code of Criminal Procedure, 1973 (CrPC) - Section 9(1), Code of Criminal Procedure, 1973 (CrPC) - Section 26, Code of Criminal Procedure, 1973 (CrPC) - Section 26(b), Code of Criminal Procedure, 1973 (CrPC) - Section 167, Code of Criminal Procedure, 1973 (CrPC) - Section 167(2), Code of Criminal Procedure, 1973 (CrPC) - Section 173, Code of Criminal Procedure, 1973 (CrPC) - Section 209, Code of Criminal Procedure, 1973 (CrPC) - Section 260(1), Code of Criminal Procedure, 1973 (CrPC) - Section 262, Code of Criminal Procedure, 1973 (CrPC) - Section 263, Code of Criminal Procedure, 1973 (CrPC) - Section 264, Code of Criminal Procedure, 1973 (CrPC) - Section 265, Code of Criminal Procedure, 1973 (CrPC) - Section 299, Code of Criminal Procedure, 1973 (CrPC) - Section 406; Constitution of India - Article 21; Explosive Substances Act, 1908 - Section 3, Explosive Substances Act, 1908 - Section 4, Explosive Substances Act, 1908 - Section 5, Explosive Substances Act, 1908 - Section 6; Indian Penal Code, 1860 (IPC) - Section 34, Indian Penal Code, 1860 (IPC) - Section 302, Indian Penal Code, 1860 (IPC) - Section 307, Indian Penal Code, 1860 (IPC) - Section 341, Indian Penal Code, 1860 (IPC) - Section 427, Indian Penal Code, 1860 (IPC) - Section 452; National Investigation Agency Act 2008 - Section 2(g), National Investigation Agency

Act 2008 - Section 2(h), National Investigation Agency Act 2008 - Section 3, National Investigation Agency Act 2008 - Section 6, National Investigation Agency Act 2008 - Section 10, National Investigation Agency Act 2008 - Section 11

No. of pages of the Original Judgement: 22

Citation: (2020)10SCC616, MANU/SC/0749/2020

Case Note: Criminal - Default Bail -Section 167(2) of the Code of Criminal Procedure, 1963 (CrPC) - First Information Report (FIR) registered against Appellant - Sections 302, 307, 452, 427, 341, 34 of the Indian Penal Code, 1860 read with Section 25 of the Arms Act, 1959, Sections 3, 4, 5, 6 of the Explosive Substances Act, 1908 and Section 13 of the Unlawful Activities (Prevention) Act, 1967 (UAPA)- No chargesheet filed after 90 days of custody - Application seeking default bail dismissed by Magistrate on the ground that 90 days' time being extended to 180 days - Special Court in appeal set aside the order for want of jurisdiction - High Court vide impugned judgment confirmed powers of Magistrate to extend the time - It was held that in case investigation is done by State police, the Magistrate empowered to extend the period of investigation upto 180 days - Hence, the present appeal

Facts: The present case pertains to claim of default which was denied to the Appellant. The appellant was apprehended in FIR registered under Sections 302, 307, 452, 427, 341, 34 of the Indian Penal Code, 1860 read with Section 25 of the Arms Act, 1959, Sections 3, 4, 5, 6 of the Explosive Substances Act, 1908 and Section 13 of the Unlawful Activities (Prevention) Act, 1967 (UAPA). Appellant remained in custody and no charge sheet was filed within 90 days, as stipulated in law. Appellant moved default bail application which was rejected by Sub-Divisional Magistrate on the ground of time being extended to 180 days. An appeal was preferred before the Special Court which set aside the order on the ground that any extension of time could be granted by it and not the Court of Sub Divisional Magistrate for want of jurisdiction. High Court however reversed the finding on the ground that Magistrate is empowered to extend the time in the circumstances of present case as investigation was being conducted by State Police and therefore case can be committed to Sessions Court. Hence, the present appeal.

Hon'ble Apex Court Held, while dismissing the Appeals: A conspectus of the aforesaid decisions would show that so long as an application for grant of default bail is made on expiry of the period of 90 days (which application need not even be in writing) before a charge sheet is filed, the right to default bail becomes complete. It is of no moment that the Criminal Court in question either does not dispose of such application before the charge sheet is filed or disposes of such application wrongly before such charge sheet is filed. So long as an application has been made for default bail on expiry of the stated period before time is further extended to the maximum period of 180 days, default bail, being an indefeasible right of the Accused under the first proviso to Section 167(2), kicks in and must be granted.

High Court wholly incorrect in stating that once the challan was presented by the prosecution on 25.03.2019 as an application was filed by the Appellant on 26.03.2019, the Appellant is not entitled to default bail. First and foremost, the High Court has got the dates all wrong. The application that was made for default bail was made on or before 25.02.2019 and not 26.03.2019. The charge sheet was filed on 26.03.2019 and not 25.03.2019. The fact that this application was wrongly dismissed on 25.02.2019 would make no difference and ought to have been corrected in revision. The sole ground for dismissing the application was that the time of 90 days had already been extended by the learned Sub-Divisional Judicial Magistrate, Ajnala by his order dated 13.02.2019. This Order was correctly set aside by the Special Court by its judgment dated 25.03.2019, holding that under the UAPA read with the NIA Act, the Special Court alone had jurisdiction to extend time to 180 days under the first proviso in Section 43-D(2)(b). The fact that the Appellant filed yet another application for default bail on 08.04.2019, would not mean that this application would wipe out the effect of the earlier application that had been wrongly decided. The right to default bail are not mere statutory rights under the first proviso to Section 167(2) of the Code, but is part of the procedure established by law Under Article 21 of the Constitution of India, which is, therefore, a fundamental right granted to an Accused person to be released on bail once the conditions of the first proviso to Section 167(2) are fulfilled.

Appeal allowed and the impugned judgment of the High Court set aside.

TEN

Virupakshappa Gouda and Ors.Vs. The State of Karnataka and Ors., 2017

Hon'ble Judges/Coram: Dipak Misra and A.M. Khanwilkar, JJ.

Act/ Sections: Prevention of Corruption Act, 1988 - Section 13(1), Prevention of Corruption Act, 1988 - Section 13(2); Indian Penal Code, 1860 (IPC) - Section 109, Indian Penal Code, 1860 (IPC) - Section 114, Indian Penal Code, 1860 (IPC) - Section 143, Indian Penal Code, 1860 (IPC) - Section 147, Indian Penal Code, 1860 (IPC) - Section 148, Indian Penal Code, 1860 (IPC) - Section 149, Indian Penal Code, 1860 (IPC) - Section 302, Indian Penal Code, 1860 (IPC) - Section 323, Indian Penal Code, 1860 (IPC) - Section 420B, Indian Penal Code, 1860 (IPC) - Section 468, Indian Penal Code, 1860 (IPC) - Section 471, Indian Penal Code, 1860 (IPC) - Section 504; Code of Criminal Procedure, 1973 (CrPC) - Section 161, Code of Criminal Procedure, 1973 (CrPC) - Section 439, Code of Criminal Procedure, 1973 (CrPC) - Section 439(2)

No. of pages of the Original Judgement: 07

Citation: AIR2017SC1685, (2017)5SCC406, MANU/SC/0344/2017

Case Note: Criminal - Grant of bail - Denial thereof - Trial Court declined to enlarge Appellants on bail - Though ground of parity was urged, same did not impress Court - High Court did not accede to prayer for grant of bail - Hence, present appeal - Whether High Court was justified in denying bail to Appellants.

Facts: A criminal case was registered against the Appellants/Accused for the offences punishable Under Sections 143, 147, 148, 323, 302, 504, 114 read with Section 149 of the Indian Penal Code, 1860. They preferred an application Under Section 439 of the Code of Criminal Procedure, 1973 for grant of bail in the court of Principal Sessions Judge, which stood dismissed. The Appellants moved the High Court. The High Court adverted to the deadly weapons that were carried by the Accused persons, the nature of injuries sustained on the vital parts by the deceased and the allegation of specific overt acts, and rejected the application. A second application for grant of bail was moved by the Appellants before the Principal Sessions Judge. The Trial Judge referred to the allegations made in the FIR, the materials that had come on record during the investigation and the postmortem report and considering all other relevant aspects, declined to enlarge the Appellants on bail. Though a ground of parity was urged on the base that the Accused Nos. 4 to 7 had been released on anticipatory bail, the same did not impress the Court and accordingly the inevitable result, the dismissal, followed. The High Court, after referring to the nature of alleged assault by the Accused persons, the type of injury sustained by the deceased and considering the pertinent facts did not accede to the prayer for grant of bail. After dismissal of the Special Leave Petition, the present appeal was filed by the Appellants.

Hon'ble Apex Court Held, while dismissing the appeal: (i) A bail application cannot be allowed solely or exclusively on the ground that the fundamental principle of criminal jurisprudence is that the Accused is presumed to be innocent till he is found guilty by the competent court. A bail application is not to be entertained on the basis of certain observations made in a different context. There has to be application of mind and appreciation of the factual score and understanding of the pronouncements in the field. An order of bail cannot be granted in an arbitrary or fanciful manner.

(ii) The Trial Judge had not been guided by the established parameters for grant of bail. He had not kept himself alive to the fact that twice the bail applications had been rejected and the matter had travelled to this Court. Once this Court has declined to enlarge the Appellants on bail, endeavours to project same factual score should not have been allowed. It is absolute impropriety and that impropriety call for axing of the order. It was not a case where the Trial Court could have entertained a bail application by elaborate dissection of facts and appreciation of statements recorded Under Section 161 Code of Criminal Procedure. The High Court performed its legal duty by lancinating the order passed by the Trial Judge.

ELEVEN

M. Radha Hari Seshu Vs. The State of Telangana, 2020

Hon'ble Judges/Coram: Ashok Bhushan and R. Subhash Reddy, JJ.

Code of Criminal Procedure, 1973 (CrPC) - Section 389(1); Indian Penal Code, 1860 (IPC) - Section 302, Indian Penal Code, 1860 (IPC) - Section 304B, Indian Penal Code, 1860 (IPC) - Section 498A.

No. of pages of the Original Judgement: 04

Citation: AIR2020SC4154, (2020)8SCC114, MANU/SC/0590/2020

Case Note: Criminal - Suspension of sentence - Sections 302, 304B and 498A of Indian Penal Code, 1860 - Case was registered against Appellant and his parents for alleged offences under Sections 498A, 304B and 302 of Code - After completion of investigation, chargesheet was filed against the Appellant-Accused No. 1, and his parents - Accused Nos. 2 and 3 for offence under Sections 304B and 498A of Code - Court of Sessions had convicted Appellant for offence under Sections 304B and 498A of Code - Accused Nos. 2 and 3 in said case were discharged - Appellant had preferred appeal before High Court seeking suspension of sentence and to release Appellant on bail, pending disposal of criminal appeal - Such application filed by Appellant was dismissed by High Court - Hence, present appeal - Whether it was fit case to suspend sentence imposed on Appellant pending Criminal Appeal before High Court.

Facts: Based on the complaint filed by the de facto complainant a case was registered against the Appellant and his parents for the alleged offences under Sections 498A, 304B and 302, Indian Penal Code (IPC). After completion of investigation, chargesheet was filed against the Appellant-Accused No. 1, and his parents - Accused Nos. 2 and 3 for the offence under Sections 304B and 498A, Indian Penal Code. The Metropolitan Magistrate took cognizance of the case against the Accused for the offences under Sections 304B and 498A, Indian Penal Code and committed it to the Court of Sessions. The Additional District and Sessions Judge had convicted the Appellant for offence under Sections 304B and 498A of Indian Penal Code. Accused Nos. 2 and 3 in the said case were discharged on an application filed by them, as such, Appellant alone was tried for the offence under Sections 498A and 304B Indian Penal Code. The Appellant had preferred appeal before the High Court seeking suspension of sentence and to release the Appellant on bail, pending disposal of the criminal appeal. Such application filed by the Appellant was dismissed by the High Court.

Hon'ble Apex Court Held, while allowing the appeal: (i) It was to be noted that marriage of the deceased with Appellant was performed and they were blessed with two children. Though initially case was registered under Sections 304B, 498A and 302, Indian Penal Code, after investigation the Appellant and his parents were charged under Sections 304B and 498A, Indian Penal Code. The parents of the Appellant were discharged on an application and only Appellant was tried for the offence under Sections 498A and 304B, Indian Penal Code. It was also brought to our notice that the Appellant was confined in jail and further it was also brought to our notice that the father of the Appellant was diagnosed with pancolitis.

(ii) Though Counsel of Appellant, by taking this court to the findings recorded by the trial court, had submitted that no case was made out for the offence under Section 304B and he was erroneously convicted for offence under Section 304B as well as 498A, Indian Penal Code, in view of the pendency of the appeal before the High Court, this court did not wish to go into the merits of the matter at this stage. Therefore, deem it appropriate that it was a fit case to suspend the sentence imposed on the Appellant and to enlarge the Appellant on bail, pending Criminal Appeal before the High Court.

TWELVE

MAHENDRA SINGH AND ORS. VS. STATE OF RAJASTHAN, 2015

Hon'ble Judges/Coram: Dipak Misra and Prafulla C. Pant, JJ.

Act/ Sections: Juvenile Justice (Care and Protection of Children) Act, 2000 [Repealed] - Section 2, Juvenile Justice (Care and Protection of Children) Act, 2000 [Repealed] - Section 20; Juvenile Justice Act, 1986 [Repealed]; Indian Penal Code, 1860 (IPC) - Section 147, Indian Penal Code, 1860 (IPC) - Section 148, Indian Penal Code, 1860 (IPC) - Section 149, Indian Penal Code, 1860 (IPC) - Section 302; Code of Criminal Procedure, 1973 (CrPC) - Section 173(8)

No. of pages of the Original Judgement: 04

Citation: (2016)16SCC312, MANU/SC/1414/2015

Case Note: Criminal - Benefit of Section 20, Juvenile Justice Act, 2000 - Determination of juvenility even after conviction - FIR filed against accused persons - Commission of murder - Chargesheet under Sections 147, 148, 302 read with Section 149, Indian Penal Code - On completion of investigation, another chargesheet filed - Two Sessions cases registered - Present Appellants - Convicts in Sessions Cases under Section 148 and 302 read with 149 Indian Penal Code - Separate appeals filed before High Court - Dismissed - Dismissal challenged in the instant appeals - Appellant Mahendra Singh contended - Benefit of Juvenile Justice Act, 2000 be extended to him - Whether the Appellant Mahendra Singh is entitled to the benefit of Section 20 of Juvenile Justice Act, 2000, though he was aged above sixteen years but less than eighteen years on the date of incident and not a juvenile under the

Juvenile Justice Act, 1986 - Whether the Lower Courts erred in convicting the Appellant Ram Singh

Facts: PW-2 gave a First Information Report at the police station that on the day of incident, accused persons have committed murder of his cousin in the field. After investigation, first charge sheet was filed against accused persons, namely, Maduram, Dalip, Mahendra Singh, Shakuntala Devi and Shyobai for their trial in respect of offences punishable Under Sections 147, 148, 302 read with Section 149 of Indian Penal Code (Indian Penal Code). The investigation against accused Ram Singh, Gyarasi Devi, Roshan, Jagat Singh and Krishna Kumar continued Under Section 173(8) of Code of Criminal Procedure, 1973, as they could not be arrested.

On completion of investigation, another charge-sheet was filed against them. From the first charge sheet, i.e. one filed against accused Dalip and others after committal, Sessions Case No. 4 of 1998 was registered, and from the another charge sheet, Sessions Case No. 95 of 2002 was registered. Since the accused were in jail, Sessions Case No. 4 of 1998 got concluded before subsequent charge was filed, and was decided. Another Session Case No. 95 of 2002 subsequently committed and registered, proceeded after the decision in the matter of first set of accused. Evidence of witnesses in the two cases was recorded separately and both were decided independently.

Present Appellants before the Court are Mahendra Singh, one of the convicts in Sessions Case No. 4 of 1998, and Ram Singh, one of the convicts in Sessions Case No. 95 of 2002. They stood convicted Under Sections 148 and 302 read with Section 149 Indian Penal Code. These two convicts filed separate appeals (along with other co-convicts) before the High Court. Both the appeals were heard together and dismissed by the High Court qua present Appellants. However, appeals of Shyobai and Shakuntala Devi were allowed and they were acquitted of the charge. Appeals of Dalip and Maduram stood abated as they died in jail. The present appeal challenges the dismissal of appeals of the present Appellants by the High Court.

Hon'ble Apex Court Held, while disposing of the appeals: 1. On behalf of the Appellant Mahendra Singh, only point argued before this Court is that, it is apparent from the lower Court record that the Appellant was aged 17 years on the date of the incident and that he has already underwent imprisonment of more than ten years. The Court's attention was drawn to the case of Hari Ram v. State of Rajasthan and Anr. and it is contended that the benefit of Juvenile Justice (Care and Protection of Children) Act, 2000 (Juvenile Justice Act, 2000) should be extended to the convict Mahendra Singh, though he was aged above sixteen years but less than eighteen years on the date of incident and not a juvenile under the Juvenile Justice Act, 1986. Since it is not disputed that Appellant Mahendra Singh was less than eighteen years of age on the date of incident, as such, the Court agrees with the argument advanced on behalf of the Appellant Mahendra Singh that he is entitled to the benefit of Section 20 of Juvenile Justice Act, 2000, as it stands today.

2. On behalf of the Appellant Ram Singh it is pointed out that the sole eye witness of the alleged incident PW-2 has assigned no role to Ram Singh. The Court went through the copy of the statement of witness PW-2, examined in subsequent Sessions Case, and found that he has nowhere stated that Ram Singh was present at the place of incident or that he assaulted the deceased. In his statement recorded, the sole eye witness has named all the accused except Ram Singh. On careful scrutiny of the evidence of sole eye witness PW-2, the Court finds that the trial Court as well as the High Court, has erred in law in concluding that the charge against accused Ram Singh stood proved on the record.

3. Therefore, the Court is of the view that the Criminal Appeal filed by Ram Singh, deserves to be allowed. Accordingly, the same is allowed and conviction recorded against him by the trial court and affirmed by the High Court is set aside. He is on bail and need not surrender.

4. As far as Appellant Mahendra Singh is concerned, the Court has already discussed that learned Counsel for said Appellant confined his submissions only regarding entitlement of benefit of Section 20 of Juvenile Justice Act, 2000, as it stands today. Following Hari Ram v. State of Rajasthan and Anr., the Court is of the opinion, that he (Mahendra Singh) is entitled to the benefit. As such, while maintaining the conviction of said Appellant Mahendra Singh, the Court sets aside the sentence awarded against him. To that extent the impugned order stands modified.

THIRTEEN

MUKESH AND ORS. VS. STATE FOR NCT OF DELHI AND ORS., 2017

Hon'ble Judges/Coram: Dipak Misra, Ashok Bhushan and R. Banumathi, JJ.

Act/ Sections: INDIAN PENAL CODE, 1860 (IPC) - Section 120B; INDIAN PENAL CODE, 1860 (IPC) - Section 201; INDIAN PENAL CODE, 1860 (IPC) - Section 302; INDIAN PENAL CODE, 1860 (IPC) - Section 307; INDIAN PENAL CODE, 1860 (IPC) - Section 365; INDIAN PENAL CODE, 1860 (IPC) - Section 366; INDIAN PENAL CODE, 1860 (IPC) - Section 376(2)(g); INDIAN PENAL CODE, 1860 (IPC) - Section 377; INDIAN PENAL CODE, 1860 (IPC) - Section 395; INDIAN PENAL CODE, 1860 (IPC) - Section 397; INDIAN PENAL CODE, 1860 (IPC) - Section 412; CODE OF CRIMINAL PROCEDURE, 1973 (CrPC) - Section 235; CODE OF CRIMINAL PROCEDURE, 1973 (CrPC) - Section 354

No. of pages of the Original Judgement: 148

Citation: AIR2017SC2161, (2017)6SCC1, MANU/SC/0575/2017

Case Note: Criminal - Capital punishment - Gang rape - Rarest of rare category - Sections 120B, 201, 302, 307, 365, 366, 376(2)(g), 377, 395, 397 and 412 of Indian Penal Code, 1860 and Sections 235 and 354 of Code of Criminal Procedure, 1973 - Deceased prosecutrix and informant boarded bus - Accused persons started to abuse informant and assaulted him with iron rods - Robbed their articles - Prosecutrix was raped by them, one after other - Prosecutrix was also subjected to unnatural sex - Her private parts and her internal organs were seriously injured - Accused were exhorting that both victims be not left alive - Threw them out of moving bus - Victims were taken to Hospital - First Information Report was registered - 1st Accused was arrested - Personal search was conducted and his disclosure statement - Investigating Officer seized bus - Arrest of 1st Accused, led to arrest of 4th and 5th Accused - Later on, 2nd Accused was apprehended - Mobile belonging to informant was recovered - In Test Identification Parade, informant identified 2nd Accused - Further recoveries were made - Dying declaration of prosecutrix was recorded - Prosecutrix gave her statement through gestures and writings - Later on, in foreign hospital, prosecutrix died - Charge-sheet came to be filed under provisions of Code, 1860 - Supplementary chargesheet was filed later on - During course of trial, 1st Accused committed suicide - Sessions Judge convicted all Accused persons under Sections 120B, 365, 366, 307, 376(2)(g), 377, 302, 395, 397, 201 and 412 - All Accused were sentenced to death for offence - Punishment of imprisonment was also awarded - Fine was also imposed - High Court affirmed conviction and confirmed death penalty - Hence, present appeals by all Accused/Appellants - Whether Accused persons were guilty of their culpability or there was public pressure, as alleged, to falsely implicate them - Whether Courts below did not follow fundamental norms of sentencing and were not guided by paramount beacons of legislative policy discernible from Sections 354(3) and 235(2) of Code, 1973 - Whether there was violation of mandate of Section 235(2) of Code, 1973 - Whether present case could be one of rarest of rare cases warranting death penalty

Facts: On 16.12.2012, the prosecution case, as projected, was that the deceased prosecutrix had gone with her friend/the informant/P.W. 1 to watch a movie. After the show was over, they took an auto and reached bus stand wherefrom they boarded a white coloured chartered bus which was bound to Dwarka/Palam Road, as a boy in the bus was calling for commuters for the said destination. As per the version of the informant, the friend of the prosecutrix, the bus had yellow and green lines/stripes and the word "Yadav" was written on it. After both of them had entered the bus, they noticed that six persons were already inside the bus, four in the cabin of the driver and two behind the driver's cabin. The deceased and the informant sat on the left side in the row of two-seaters and paid the fare. The Accused persons did not allow anyone else to board and the bus moved and the lights inside the bus were put off. The lights were put off. A few minutes later, three Accused persons, including a juvenile in conflict with law, came out of the driver's cabin and started to abuse the informant, who raised opposition to the abuse that led to an altercation which invited the other two who were sitting outside the driver's cabin to join. He was assaulted by the Accused persons with the iron rods that caused injuries to his head, both the legs and other parts of the body and the consequence was that he fell on the floor of the bus. The two Accused persons pinned the informant down and robbed the victims of their mobiles besides robbing the informant of his purse, clothes and other articles. As per the version of the prosecution, the informant was carrying two mobiles and the prosecutrix was carrying only one, and the Accused snatched away all the three mobiles. The Accused persons took the prosecutrix to the rear side of the bus and she was raped by them, one after the other. The prosecutrix was also subjected to unnatural sex. Her private parts and her internal organs were seriously injured. The prosecutrix was carrying a grey colour purse. The Accused persons robbed her of her belongings and stripped her. They also took away the clothes of the informant while beating him with iron rods. The Accused were exhorting that both the victims be not left alive. The Accused then tried to throw both the informant and the prosecutrix out of the moving bus from its rear door but could not open it and so, they brought them to the front door and threw them out of the moving bus at National Highway No. 8, Hotel Delhi 37, Mahipalpur flyover by the side of the road.

The prosecutrix and the informant were noticed by P.W. 72, who heard the voice of the prosecutrix. P.W. 72 saw the informant and the prosecutrix sitting naked having blood all around. Immediately thereafter, P.W. 72 informed P.W. 70, who was in the Control Room, requesting him to call PCR. P.W. 70 dialed 100 No. and even asked his other patrolling staff to reach the spot. P.W. 73/H.C., who was in charge of PCR van Zebra 54, received information about the incident and the lying of victims in a naked condition. P.W. 73 reached the spot and found the victims. He got the crowd dispersed and brought a bottle of water and a bedsheet from the nearby hotel and tore the same into two parts and gave it to both the victims to cover themselves. P.W. 73 took the victims to Safdarjung Hospital. On the way to the hospital, the victims gave their names to him and informed about the incident. While leaving the informant in the casualty where he was examined by P.W. 51 and his MLC/P.W. 51/A, was drawn up, P.W. 73 took the prosecutrix to the Gynae ward and got her admitted there. The MLC of the prosecutrix, P.W. 49/B, was prepared by P.W. 49, who recorded the history of the incident as told to her by the prosecutrix and noted the same in Exhibit P.W. 49/A.

After the victims were rescued, the informant gave his first statement to the police at 3:45 a.m. on 17.12.2012 which culminated into the recording of the FIR at 5:40 a.m. being FIR No. 413/2012 Under Section 120B of Indian Penal Code and Sections 365/366/376(2)(g)/377/307/302 of Indian Penal Code, 1860 and/or Sections 396/395 of Indian Penal Code, 1860 read with Sections 397/201/412 of Indian Penal Code, 1860. It was thereafter handed over to P.W. 80 for investigation. On the same night, i.e., 16/17.12.2012, the prosecutrix underwent first surgery. The prosecutrix was operated by P.W. 50. The second and third surgeries were performed on 19.12.2012 and 23.12.2012 respectively.

On 17.12.2012, supplementary statements of the informant were recorded by P.W. 80. Based on the description of the bus given by the informant, the offending bus was found parked in Ravi Das Jhuggi Camp, R.K. Puram, New Delhi. P.W. 80 along with P.W. 74/SI and P.W. 65/Ct., went to the spot and found 1st Accused sitting in the bus. On seeing the police, 1st Accused got down from the bus and started running. The police intercepted 1st Accused and he was arrested and interrogated.

Personal search was conducted on 1st Accused and his disclosure statement, Ex. P-74/F, was recorded by P.W. 74 and his team. Based on his disclosure statement, P.W. 74 Investigating Officer seized the bus, Ex. P1, vide Seizure Memo Ex. P.W. 74/K. P.W. 74 seized the seat cover of the bus of red colour and its curtains of yellow colour. On the bus, 'Yadav' was found written on its body with green and yellow stripes on it. The Investigating Officer also seized the key of the bus, Ex. P-74/2, vide Seizure Memo Ex. P.W. 74/J. The documents of the bus were also seized. The disclosure statement of 1st Accused, Ex. P.W. 74/F, led to the recovery of his bloodstained clothes, iron rods and debit card of the mother of the prosecutrix. P.W. 74, Investigating Officer, also recovered ashes and the partly unburnt clothes lying near the bus which was seized vide Memo Exhibit No. P.W. 74/M and Unix Mobile Phone with MTNL Sim, Ex. P-74/5, vide Memo Ex. P/74E. The Investigating Officer prepared the site plan of the place where the bus was parked and from where the ashes were found.

The arrest of 1st Accused also led to the arrest of 4th Accused and 5th Accused. On 18.12.2012, 2nd Accused was apprehended by P.W. 58/SI and was produced before P.W. 80. At the instance of 2nd Accused, a Samsung Galaxy Trend DUOS Blue Black mobile belonging to the informant was recovered. On 23.12.2012, at his instance, P.W. 80 prepared the route chart of the route where 2nd Accused drove the bus at the time of the incident, Ex. P.W. 80/H. Besides that, he got recovered his bloodstained clothes from the garage of his brother. He opted to undergo Test Identification Parade (TIP). In the Test Identification Parade conducted by P.W. 17/Metropolitan Magistrate, the informant identified 2nd Accused. 5th Accused was apprehended and arrested about 1:15 p.m. on 18.12.2012 vide memo Ex. P.W. 60/A; his disclosure, Ex. P.W. 60/G, was recorded and his personal search was conducted vide memo Ex. P.W. 60/C. In his disclosure statement, 5th Accused pointed out Munirka bus stand where the prosecutrix and the informant boarded the bus and memo Ex. P.W. 68/I was prepared. He also pointed at the spot where the informant and the prosecutrix were thrown out of the bus and memo Ex. P.W. 68/J was prepared in this regard.

4th Accused got recovered his bloodstained clothes, the informant's leather shoes and the prosecutrix's mobile phone, Nokia Model 3110 of black grey colour. Further recoveries were made pursuant to his supplementary disclosure. Similarly, 5th Accused got recovered his bloodstained clothes, shoes and also a wrist watch make Sonata and Rs. 1000/- robbed from the informant.

3rd Accused was also arrested from a village of Bihar. His disclosure statement was recorded. He led to his brother's house and got recovered his bloodstained clothes. A ring belonging to the informant, two metro cards and a Nokia phone with SIM of Vodafone Company was also recovered from 3rd Accused. 3rd Accused also opted to undergo TIP and was positively identified by the informant. The mobile phones of the Accused persons were seized and call details records with requisite certificates Under Section 65-B of Indian Evidence Act were obtained by the police. After getting arrested, all the Accused were medically examined. The MLCs of all the Accused persons showed various injuries on their person; viz., in the MLC, Ex. P.W. 2/A, of 1st Accused, P.W. 2 opined that the injuries could possibly be struggle marks. Similar opinions were received in respect of other Accused persons.

The prosecutrix was re-operated on 23.12.2012 for peritoneal lavage and placement of drain under general anaesthesia and the notes are exhibited as Ex. P.W. 50/E. As the condition of the prosecutrix did not improve much, the prosecution thought it appropriate to record the statements of the prosecutrix. The said statements were conferred the status of dying declaration. P.W. 49 also deposed that certain exhibits were collected for examination such as outer clothes. On 21.12.2012, on being declared fit, the second dying declaration was recorded by P.W. 27/Sub-Divisional Magistrate. This dying declaration was an elaborate one where the prosecutrix described the incident in detail. She also stated that the accused were addressing each other with names. On 25th December, 2012, P.W. 30/ Metropolitan Magistrate, went to the hospital to record the dying declaration of the prosecutrix. The attending doctors opined that the prosecutrix was not in a position to speak but she was otherwise conscious and responded by way of gestures. Accordingly, P.W. 30 put questions in such a manner as to enable her to narrate the incident by way of gestures or writing. Her statement, Ex. P.W. 30/D, was recorded by P.W. 30 in the form of dying declaration by putting her questions in the nature of multiple-choice questions. The prosecutrix gave her statement/dying declaration through gestures and writings, Exhibit P.W. 30/D.

Since the condition of the prosecutrix was critical, it was decided that she be shifted abroad for further treatment and fostering oasis of hope on 27th December, 2012, she was shifted to a Hospital of Singapore, for her further treatment. The hope and expiration became a visible mirage as the prosecutrix died on 29th December, 2012. P.W. 34/Forensic Pathologist deposed that her exact time of death was 4:45 a.m. on 29th December, 2012. The cause of her death was sepsis with multiple organ failure following multiple injuries. The original post mortem report was Ex. P.W. 34/A and its scanned copy is Ex. P.W. 34/B; the Toxicology Report dated 4th January, 2013 was Exhibit P.W. 34/C. In the post-mortem report, Ex. P.W. 34/A, besides other serious injuries, various bite marks were observed.

The investigating agency went around to collect the electronic evidence. A CCTV footage produced by P.W. 25 in a CD, Ex. P.W. 25/C-1 and P.W. 25/ C-2, and the photographs, Ex. P.W. 25/B-1 to Ex. P.W. 25/B-7, were collected to ascertain the presence of the informant and the prosecutrix at the Mall. The certificate Under Section 65-B of the Indian Evidence Act, 1872 with respect to the said footage was proved by P.W. 26 vide Ex. P.W. 26/A. Another important evidence was the CCTV footage of Hotel Delhi 37 situated near the dumping spot. The said footage showed a bus matching the description given by the informant and said bus had the word "Yadav" written on one side. Thereafter, the report of the CFSL was received.

The report, after analysing the DNA profiles generated from the known samples of the prosecutrix, the informant, and each of the Accused, concluded that the samples were authentic and established the identities of the persons beyond reasonable doubt. P.W. 46/Senior Scientific Officer (Finger Prints) submitted his report Ex. P.W. 46/D. In the report, the chance prints of 4th Accused were found to have matched with those on the bus in question. Bite mark analysis was also undertaken by the investigative team to establish the identity and involvement of the Accused persons. P.W. 66 had taken 10 photographs of different parts of the body of the prosecutrix which were marked as Ex. P.W. 66/B (Colly.) and Ex. P.W. 66/C (Colly.). P.W. 66 also proved in Court the certificate provided by him in terms of Section 65-B of the Evidence Act in respect of the photographs, Ex. P.W. 66/A. Thereafter, P.W. 18 collected the photographs and the dental models from Safdarjung Hospital and duly deposited the same in the malkhana after he, P.W. 18, had handed them over to the S.H.O/P.W. 78. The same were later entrusted to S.I./P.W. 18. P.W. 71 submitted the final report in this regard which is exhibited as Ex. P.W. 71/C. In the said report, he concluded that at least three bite marks were caused by 1st Accused whereas one bite mark was identified to have been most likely caused by 3rd Accused. The chargesheet came to be filed Under Section 365/376(2)(g)/377/307/395/397/302/396/412/201/120/34 of Indian Penal Code, 1860 and supplementary chargesheet was filed later. During trial, 1st Accused committed suicide and the proceedings qua him stood abated. Sessions Judge convicted all the Accused persons Under Section 120B Indian Penal Code for the offence of criminal conspiracy; Under Section 365/366 Indian Penal Code read with Section 120B Indian Penal Code for abducting the victims with an intention to force the prosecutrix to illicit intercourse; Under Section 307 Indian Penal Code read with Section 120B Indian Penal Code for attempting to kill the informant; Under Section 376(2)(g) Indian Penal Code for committing gang rape with the prosecutrix in pursuance of their conspiracy; Under Section 377 Indian Penal Code read with Section 120B Indian Penal Code for committing unnatural offence with the prosecutrix; Under Section 302 Indian Penal Code read with Section 120B Indian Penal Code for committing murder of the helpless prosecutrix; Under Section 395 Indian Penal Code for conjointly committing dacoity in pursuance of the aforesaid conspiracy; Under Section 397 Indian Penal Code read with Section 120B Indian Penal Code for the use of iron rods and for attempting to kill the informant at the time of committing robbery; Under Section 201 Indian Penal Code read with Section 120B Indian Penal Code for destroying of evidence and Under Section 412 Indian Penal Code for the offence of being individually found in possession of the stolen property which they all knew was a stolen booty of dacoity committed by them. All the Accused were sentenced to death for offence punishable Under Section 302 Indian Penal Code and for other offences, punishment of imprisonment of different duration was awarded. Fine was also imposed and in default of payment of fine such convict shall undergo simple imprisonment for a period of one month. The sentences Under Sections 120B/365/366/376(2)(g)/377/201/395/397/412 Indian Penal Code were directed to run concurrently and that the benefit Under Section 428 Code of Criminal Procedure would be given wherever applicable.

The High Court affirmed the conviction and confirmed the death penalty imposed upon the Accused by expressing the opinion that under the facts and circumstances of the case, imposition of death penalty awarded by the Trial Court deserved to be confirmed in respect of all the four Accused. As the death penalty was confirmed, the appeals preferred by the Accused were dismissed.

Hon'ble Apex Court Held, while dismissing the appeals:

Dipak Misra, J.: (i) There was no delay in the registration of FIR. The sequence of events were natural. After the occurrence, the victim was seriously injured and was in a critical condition and it had to be treated as a natural conduct that giving medical treatment to her was of prime importance. The admission of the informant and the victim in the hospital and the completion of procedure must have taken some time. The informant himself was injured and was admitted to the hospital. No delay could be said to have been caused in examining the informant. It is not expected from a victim to give details of the incident either in the FIR or in the brief history given to the doctors. If any overt act is attributed to a particular accused among the assailants, it must be given greater assurance. The involvement of the Accused persons could not be determined solely on the basis of what was mentioned in the FIR. The informant stated about the presence of four persons sitting in the cabin of the bus and two boys sitting behind the cabin and clearly stated about the overt act. He broadly made reference to the Accused persons and also to the overt acts. There were no indications of fabrication in the statement of the informant. It could not be said that merely because the names of the Accused persons were not mentioned in the FIR, it raised serious doubts about the prosecution case.

(ii) The contentions assailing the evidence of the informant did not merit acceptance, for at the time when he was first examined his friend/the prosecutrix was critically injured and he was in a shocked mental condition. The evidence of a witness is not to be disbelieved simply because he is a partisan witness or related to the prosecution. It is to be weighed whether he was present or not and whether he is telling the truth or not. The informant clearly spoken about the occurrence and also corroborated his complaint. The injuries found on the person of the informant and the fact that the informant was injured in the same occurrence lent assurance to his testimony that he was present at the time of the occurrence along with the prosecutrix. The evidence of an injured witness is entitled to a greater weight and the testimony of such a witness is considered to be beyond reproach and reliable. Firm, cogent and convincing ground is required to discard the evidence of an injured witness. It is to be kept in mind that the evidentiary value of an injured witness carries great weight. Apart from the injuries sustained, the presence of the informant was further confirmed by the DNA analysis.

(iii) The evidence of the informant was not to be disbelieved simply because there were certain omissions. The Accused persons were in a group and were also armed with iron rods. The informant was held by them. It would not have been possible for the informant to resist the number of Accused persons and save the prosecutrix. The evidence of the informant could not be doubted on the ground that he had not interfered with the occurrence. The improvements made in the supplementary statement need not necessarily render the informant's evidence untrustworthy more so when the informant had no reason to falsely implicate the Accused.

(iv) Once it is proved before the Court through the testimony of the experts that the photographs and the CCTV footage are not tampered with, there is no reason or justification to perceive the same with the lens of doubt. It was perceptible that the High Court, in order to satisfy itself, had got the CCTV footage played during the hearing and found the same to be creditworthy and acceptable. There was dearth of space inside the police stations and the use of Stadium, where the bus was taken to, as parking lot by the Police in the present case did not necessarily mean that there was any mala fide intention on the part of the investigating agency without any specific assertion to advance the said bald allegation.

(v) The contention of the Accused that the testimony of P.W. 81/the owner of the bus deserved to be totally discarded, was unacceptable. The principal contention was that P.W. 81 was in judicial custody and, therefore, his version in the Court was under tremendous pressure as he was desirous of getting a bail order to enjoy his liberty. However, it was limpid from the deposition of P.W. 81 that he was in judicial custody for a separate offence and, therefore, it was difficult to accede to the argument advanced by the Accused that he was under pressure to support the version of the prosecution. It stood proved that the bus in question was routinely driven by 1st Accused.

(vi) All the Accused persons were closely associated with each other. It was not permissible to advance an argument that Section 27 of the Evidence Act, 1872 was constantly abused by the prosecution or that it used the said provision as a lethal weapon against anyone it likes. The recoveries made when the Accused persons were in custody were established with certainty. The witnesses who deposed with regard to the recoveries remained absolutely unshaken and, in fact, nothing was elicited from them to disprove their creditworthiness. The recoveries of articles belonging to the informant and the victim from the custody of the Accused persons could not be discarded. No explanation was by the Accused persons explaining as to how they had got into possession of the said articles.

(vii) 4th Accused and 5th Accused refused to participate in the TIP proceedings without giving any reason whatsoever. The informant identified 2nd Accused and 3rd Accused. Test Identification Proceedings corroborated and lent assurance to the dock identification of 2nd Accused and 3rd Accused by the informant. The informant, apart from identifying the Accused who had made themselves available in the TIP, also identified all of them in Court. The TIP was not dented.

(viii) A dying declaration is an important piece of evidence which, if found veracious and voluntary by the court, could be the sole basis for conviction. If a dying declaration is found to be voluntary and made in fit mental condition, it can be relied upon even without any corroboration. However, the Court, while admitting a dying declaration, must be vigilant towards the need for 'Compos Mentis Certificate' from a doctor as well as the absence of any kind of tutoring. A mere omission on the part of the prosecutrix to state the entire factual details of the incident in her very first statement did not make her subsequent statements unworthy, especially when her statements were duly corroborated by other prosecution witnesses including the medical evidence. The contention that the third dying declaration made through gestures lacked credibility and that the same ought to have been videographed, was totally sans substance. The dying declaration recorded on the basis of nods and gestures is not only admissible but also possesses evidentiary value, the extent of which shall depend upon who recorded the statement. All the three dying declarations were consistent with each other and well corroborated with other evidence and the Trial Court as well as the High Court correctly placed reliance upon the dying declarations of the prosecutrix to record the conviction.

(ix) The dying declaration of the prosecutrix, which is highly reliable, clearly established the horrendous use of iron rods by the Accused persons. The factum of insertion of iron rods in the private parts of the prosecutrix was also fortified by the scientific evidence. Merely because the injuries sustained by the informant were opined to be of simple nature, the use of iron rods could not be doubted. The informant's omission to state the factum of use of iron rods in his complaint or MLC was not fatal to the case of the prosecution. Merely because no injuries to the uterus of the victim were noticed, that did not lead to the conclusion that iron rod was not used.
(x) In order to establish a clear link between the accused persons and the incident at hand, the prosecution also adduced scientific evidence in the form of DNA, fingerprint and bite mark analysis. If the quality control is maintained, it is treated to be quite accurate and as the same was established.

(xi) Forensic Odontology has established itself as an important and indispensable science in medico-legal matters and expert evidence through various reports which have been utilized by courts in the administration of justice. In the case at hand, the report was wholly credible because of matching of bite marks with the tooth structure of the Accused persons and there was no reason to view the same with any suspicion.

(xii) There existed contradictions in the statements of the defence witnesses produced on behalf of 5th Accused. It is settled in law that while raising a plea of 'alibi', the burden squarely lies upon the accused person to establish the plea convincingly by adducing cogent evidence. The plea of 'alibi' that 4th Accused and 5th Accused had attended the alleged musical programme in the evening of 16.12.2012 was rightly rejected by the Trial Court which was given the stamp of approval by the High Court.

(xiii) Conspiracy and its objective can be inferred from the surrounding circumstances and the conduct of the accused. Moreover, conspiracy being a continuing offence continues to subsist till it is executed or rescinded or frustrated by the choice of necessity. The presence of P.W. 82 in the bus prior to the boarding of the bus by the informant and the victim and the presence of all the Accused in the bus was established by the prosecution.

(xiv) The prosecution established that the Accused were associated with each other. The criminal acts done in furtherance of conspiracy was established by the sequence of events and the conduct of the Accused. The chain of events described by the prosecutrix in her dying declarations coupled with the testimonies of the other witnesses established that as soon as the informant and the prosecutrix boarded the bus, the Accused persons formed an agreement to commit heinous offences against the victim. Forcefully having sexual intercourse with the prosecutrix, one after the other, inserting iron rod in her private parts, dragging her by her hair and then throwing her out of the bus all established the common intent of the Accused to rape and murder the prosecutrix. The Trial Court rightly recorded that the prosecutrix's alimentary canal from the level of duodenum upto 5 cm of anal sphincter was completely damaged. It was beyond repair. Causing of damage to the jejunum was indicative of the fact that the rod was inserted through the vagina and/or anus upto the level of jejunum. Further, septicemia was the direct result of multiple internal injuries. Moreover, the prosecutrix also maintained in her dying declaration that the Accused persons were exhorting that the prosecutrix had died and she be thrown out of the bus. Ultimately, both the prosecutrix as well as the informant were thrown out of the moving bus through the front door by the Accused after having failed to throw them through the rear door. The conduct of the Accused in committing heinous offences with the prosecutrix in concert with each other and thereafter throwing her out of the bus in an unconscious state along with the informant unequivocally brought home the charge Under Section 120B in case of each of them. The criminal acts done in furtherance of the conspiracy was evident from the acts and also the words uttered during the commission of the offence. Therefore, the Trial court and the High Court correctly considered the entire case on the touchstone of well-recognised principles for arriving at the conclusion of criminal conspiracy. The relevant evidence on record led to a singular conclusion that the Accused persons were liable for criminal conspiracy and their confessions to counter the same deserved to be repelled.

(xv) The present Court concluded that the evidence of the informant was unimpeachable and it deserved to be relied upon. The Accused persons alongwith the juvenile in conflict with law were present in the bus when the prosecutrix and her friend got into the bus. There was no reason to disregard the CCTV footage, establishing the description and movement of the bus. The arrest of the Accused persons from various places at different times was proved by the prosecution. The personal search, recoveries and the disclosure leading to recovery were in consonance with law and the assail of the same on the counts of custodial confession made under torture and other pleas were highly specious pleas and they did not remotely create a dent in the said aspects. The contention raised by the Accused persons that the recoveries on the basis of disclosure were a gross manipulation by the investigating agency and deserved to be thrown overboard did not merit acceptance. The relationship between the parties having been clearly established, their arrest gains more credibility and the involvement of each accused gains credence. The dying declarations, three in number, do withstand close scrutiny and they were consistent with each other. The stand that the deceased could not have given any dying declaration because of her health condition has to be repelled because the witnesses who stated about the dying declarations stood embedded to their version and nothing was brought on record to discredit the same. That apart, the dying declaration by gestures was proved beyond reasonable doubt. There was no justification to think that the informant and the deceased would falsely implicate the Accused and leave the real culprits. The dying declarations made by the deceased received corroboration from the oral and documentary evidence and also enormously from the medical evidence. The DNA profiling, which was done after taking due care for quality, proved to the hilt the presence of the Accused in the bus and their involvement in the crime. The submission that certain samples were later on taken from the Accused and planted on the deceased to prove the DNA aspect was noted only to be rejected because it had no legs to stand upon. The argument that the transfusion of blood had the potentiality to give rise to two categories of DNA or two DNAs was farthest from truth and there was no evidence on that score. On the contrary, the evidence in exclusivity points to the matching of the DNA of the deceased with that of the Accused on many aspects. The evidence brought on record with regard to finger prints was absolutely impeccable and the Trial court and the High Court correctly placed reliance on the same and that there was no reason to disbelieve the same. The scientific evidence relating to odontology showed how far the Accused proceeded and where the bites were found and it was extremely impossible to accept the submission that it had been a manipulation by the investigating agency to rope in the Accused persons. The evidence brought on record as regards criminal conspiracy stands established. The brutal, barbaric and diabolic nature of the crime was evincible from the acts committed by the Accused persons. The aggravating circumstances outweigh the mitigating circumstances now brought on record. Therefore, the High Court correctly confirmed the death penalty.

R. Banumathi, J. - concurring view: (xvi) Persisting notion that the testimony of victim has to be corroborated by other evidence must be removed. To equate a rape victim to an accomplice is to add insult to womanhood. Ours is a conservative society and not a permissive society. Ordinarily a woman, more so, a young woman will not stake her reputation by levelling a false charge, concerning her chastity. It is well-settled that conviction can be based on the sole testimony of the prosecutrix if it is implicitly reliable and there is a ring of truth in it. Corroboration as a condition for judicial reliance on the testimony of a prosecutrix is not requirement of law but a guidance of prudence under given circumstances.

(xvii) In cases where there are more than one dying declarations, the Court should consider whether they are consistent with each other. If there are inconsistencies, the nature of the inconsistencies must be examined as to whether they are material or not. In cases where there is more than one dying declaration, it is the duty of the Court to consider each one of them and satisfy itself as to the voluntariness and reliability of the declarations. Mere fact of recording multiple dying declarations does not take away the importance of each individual declaration. Court has to examine the contents of dying declaration in the light of various surrounding facts and circumstances.

(xviii) When a dying declaration is recorded voluntarily, pursuant to a fitness report of a certified doctor, nothing much remains to be questioned unless, it is proved that the dying declaration was tainted with animosity and a result of tutoring. Though there was time gap between the declarations, all the three dying declarations were consistent with each other and there were no material contradictions. All the three dying declarations depicted truthful version of the incident, particularly the detailed narration of the incident concerning the rape committed on the victim, insertion of iron rod and the injuries caused to her vagina and rectum, unnatural sex committed on the victim and throwing the victim and the informant out of the moving bus. All the three dying declarations being voluntary, consistent and trustworthy, satisfied the test of reliability. The dying declarations were well-corroborated by medical and scientific evidence adduced by the prosecution. Moreover, the same was amply corroborated by the testimony of eye witness-the informant. The dying declaration is amply corroborated by medical evidence. The dying declarations well corroborated by medical and scientific evidence strengthened the case of the prosecution by conclusively connecting the Accused with the crime.

(xix) The computer generated electronic record in evidence, admissible at a trial is proved in the manner specified in Section 65B of the Evidence Act. Sub-section (1) of Section 65 of the Evidence Act makes electronic records admissible as a document, paper print out of electronic records stored in optical or magnetic media produced by a computer, subject to the fulfillment of the conditions specified in Sub-section (2) of Section 65B of the Evidence Act. When those conditions are satisfied, the electronic record becomes admissible in any proceeding without further proof or production of the original, as evidence of any of the contents of the original or any fact stated therein of which direct evidence is admissible. Secondary evidence of contents of document can also be led Under Section 65 of the Evidence Act.

(xx) Section 25 of the Indian Evidence Act speaks of a confession made to a police officer, which shall not be proved as against a person accused of an offence. Section 26 of the Evidence Act also speaks that no confession made by the person whilst he is in the custody of a police officer, unless it be made in the immediate presence of a Magistrate, shall be proved as against such person. Sections 25 and 26 of the Evidence Act put a complete bar on the admissibility of a confessional statement made to a police officer or a confession made in absentia of a Magistrate, while in custody. Section 27 of the Evidence Act is by way of a proviso to Sections 25 and 26 of the Evidence Act and a statement even by way of confession made in police custody which distinctly relates to the fact discovered is admissible in evidence against the Accused.

(xxi) DNA evidence is now a predominant forensic technique for identifying criminals when biological tissues are left at the scene of crime or for identifying the source of blood found on any articles or clothes etc. recovered from the accused or from witnesses. DNA testing on samples such as saliva, skin, blood, hair or semen not only helps to convict the accused but also serves to exonerate. Meeting of minds for committing an illegal act is sine qua non of the offence of conspiracy. It is also obvious that meeting of minds, thereby resulting in formation of a consensus between the parties, can be a sudden act, spanning in a fraction of a minute. It is neither necessary that each of the conspirators take active part in the commission of each and every conspiratorial act, nor it is necessary that all the conspirators must know each and every detail of the conspiracy.

(xxii) The most important aspect of the offence of conspiracy is that apart from being a distinct statutory offence, all the parties to the conspiracy are liable for the acts of each other and as an exception to the general law in the case of conspiracy intent i.e. mens rea alone constitutes a crime. There was ample evidence proving the acts, statements and circumstances, establishing firm ground to hold that the Accused who were present in the bus were in prior concert to commit the offence of rape. The prosecution established that the Accused were associated with each other. The criminal acts done in furtherance of conspiracy, was established by the sequence of events and the conduct of the Accused. Existence of conspiracy and its objects could be inferred from the chain of events. The chain of events described by the victim in her dying declarations coupled with the testimony of the informant established that as soon as the informant and the victim boarded the bus, the Accused switched off the lights of the bus. Few Accused pinned down the informant and others committed rape on the victim in the back side of the bus one after the other. The Accused inserted iron rods in the private parts of the prosecutrix, dragging her holding her hair and then threw her outside the bus. The victim also maintained in her dying declaration that the Accused persons were exhorting that the victim died and she be thrown out of the bus. Ultimately, both the victim and the informant were thrown out of the moving bus through the front door, having failed to throw them through the rear door. The chain of action and the act of finally throwing the victim and the informant out of the bus showed that there was unity of object among the accused to commit rape and destroy the evidence thereon.

(xxiii) Under Section 235(2) Code of Criminal Procedure, 1973 where the Accused is convicted, save in cases of admonition or release on good conduct, the Judge shall hear the Accused on the question of sentence and then pass sentence in accordance with law. Section 235(2) of Code of Criminal Procedure, 1973 imposes duty on the court to hear the Accused on the question of sentence and then pass sentence on him in accordance with law. The only exception to the said rule is created in case of applicability of Section 360 of Code of Criminal Procedure, 1973 i.e. when the court finds the Accused eligible to be released on probation of good conduct or after admonition. Section 354 of Code of Criminal Procedure, 1973 specifies the language and contents of judgment, while delivering the judgment in a criminal case. Section 354(3) of Code of Criminal Procedure, 1973 deals with judgments where conviction is for an offence punishable with death penalty or in the alternative with imprisonment for life. Section 354(3) of Code of Criminal Procedure, 1973 mandates that when the conviction is for an offence punishable with death or, in the alternative, with imprisonment for life or imprisonment for a term of years, the judgment shall state the reasons for the sentence awarded, and in the case of sentence of death, the special reasons for such sentence.

(xxiv) Where a crime is committed with extreme brutality and the collective conscience of the society is shocked, courts must award death penalty, irrespective of their personal opinion as regards desirability of death penalty. By not imposing a death sentence in such cases, the Courts may do injustice to the society at large. Diabolic nature of the crime and the manner of committing crime, as reflected in committing gang-rape with the victim; forcing her to perform oral sex, injuries on the body of the deceased by way of bite marks; insertion of iron rod in her private parts and causing fatal injuries to her private parts and other internal injuries; pulling out her internal organs which caused sepsis and ultimately led to her death; throwing the victim and the informant naked in the cold wintery night and trying to run the bus over them. The brazenness and coldness with which the acts were committed in the evening hours by picking up the deceased and the victim from a public space, reflected the threat to which the society would be posed to, in case the Accused are not appropriately punished. There was no scope of reform. The horrific acts reflecting the in-human extent to which the Accused could go to satisfy their lust, being completely oblivious, not only to the norms of the society, but also to the norms of humanity. The acts committed so shook the conscience of the society. The circumstances stated by the Accused were too slender to be treated as mitigating circumstances. Offences against women are not a women's issue alone but, human rights issue.

FOURTEEN

NARAYANA REDDY VS. STATE OF KARNATAKA, 2016

Hon'ble Judges/Coram: A.K. Sikri and R.K. Agrawal, JJ.

Act/ Sections: Indian Penal Code, 1860 (IPC) - Section 34, Indian Penal Code, 1860 (IPC) - Section 143, Indian Penal Code, 1860 (IPC) - Section 144, Indian Penal Code, 1860 (IPC) - Section 145, Indian Penal Code, 1860 (IPC) - Section 147, Indian Penal Code, 1860 (IPC) - Section 148, Indian Penal Code, 1860 (IPC) - Section 149, Indian Penal Code, 1860 (IPC) - Section 302; Code of Criminal Procedure, 1973 (CrPC) - Section 313

No. of pages of the original Judgement: 06

Citation: (2016)14SCC212, MANU/SC/0769/2016

Case Note: Criminal - Conviction - Credibility of testimony - Sections 34 and 302 of Indian Penal Code, 1860 - Complaint was lodged by Complainant/ Prosecution Witness-1 (PW-1) stating that Appellant had stabbed deceased - PW-1 named Accused Nos. 2 to 6 also - Trial Court acquitted Accused Nos. 3, 5 and 6 of all charges framed but convicted Appellant and Accused No. 2 for offence punishable under Section 302 read with Section 34 of Code - High Court acquitted Accused No. 2 and dismissed appeal of Appellant - Hence, present appeal - Whether Courts below had rightly gone by proposition that once PW-1's testimony was to be believed, ocular evidence might be singular now, which was sufficient to convict Appellant

Facts: A complaint was lodged with the Police Station by Complainant/ Prosecution Witness (PW)-1 stating that Accused No. 1/Appellant had stabbed deceased with knife. FIR to this effect was registered. In his later statements, PW-1 named Accused Nos. 2 to 6 also, who were the relatives of the Appellant. A charge-sheet was filed for offences punishable under Sections 143, 144, 145, 147, 148 and 302 read with Section 149 of the Indian Penal Code, 1860 against all the six Accused persons. The Trial Court acquitted Accused Nos. 3, 5 and 6 of all the charges framed but convicted Appellant and Accused No. 2 for the offence punishable under Section 302 read with Section 34 of Code, 1860 and acquitted them of other charges. Accused No. 4 had died during the trial and, therefore, the trial against him had abated. The High Court acquitted Accused No. 2 and dismissed the appeal of the Appellant. The appeal of Appellant was decided by present Court by remitting the matter to the High Court for fresh consideration. In the meantime, the Appellant was ordered to be released on bail. After the remittal of the case to the High Court, the High Court maintained its earlier decision. Hence, the present appeal.

Hon'ble Apex Court Held: (i) The conviction was recorded on the basis of the testimony of PW-1. The Prosecution had not been able to establish that there was sufficient light in which PW-1 could see the persons who had attacked the deceased. It was possible that PW-1 reached the spot immediately after the incident but was not there at the time of incident or if he was at a distance, he could not see who were the persons who had attacked the deceased. When he disclosed the information about the murder of deceased to the deceased's wife, he did not name anybody and on the contrary said that somebody had killed. This was what was repeated by PW-1 himself when he went to the police station and disclosed to the Head Constable present there about the incident. Thereafter in the complaint, he mentioned the name of the Appellant only. He improved upon the statement and in his subsequent statement, he implicated five more persons. The prosecution story and, in particular, the testimony of PW-1, was totally untrustworthy when it was examined the medical evidence that was the post mortem report which was produced and the opinion of the doctor who conducted the said post mortem examination thereupon.

(ii) Though recovery of the knife was done at the disclosure statement allegedly made by the Appellant, that had not been proved at all and, therefore, the prosecution did not rely thereupon. The entire prosecution allegation was shrouded in mystery which did not inspire any confidence. Even PW-1 could not be believed and it appeared that either out of suspicion or out of vengeance PW-1 had implicated the Appellant along with the other accused persons. The conviction of the Appellant was set aside.

FIFTEEN

R. Damodaran Vs. The State Represented by the Inspector of Police, 2021

Hon'ble Judges/Coram: Ashok Bhushan and Ajay Rastogi, JJ.

Act/ Sections: Code of Criminal Procedure, 1973 (CrPC) - Section 174, Code of Criminal Procedure, 1973 (CrPC) - Section 313; Indian Penal Code, 1860 (IPC) - Section 302, Indian Penal Code, 1860 (IPC) - Section 304

No. of pages of the Original Judgement: 06

Citation: AIR2021SC1173, MANU/SC/0109/2021

Case Note: Criminal - Murder - Conviction - Circumstantial Evidence-Section 302 of the Indian Penal Code, 1860 (IPC) -Appellant accused of murdering his own wife - Wife after being hit by Appellant taken to hospital citing her to have suffered cardiac arrest - Autopsy confirmed death caused due to shock and haemorrhage - Appellant prosecuted and held guilty - Hence, the present appeal - Whether Appellant rightly convicted for murdering his wife?

Facts: The Accused Appellant was convicted for offence under Section 302 of the Indian Penal Code, 1860 (IPC) for murdering his own wife while she was at the advanced stage of her pregnancy. High Court vide judgment impugned confirmed the finding of Trial Court. As alleged, Appellant used to frequently change his rented accommodation and on each change used to make deceased fetch money from her father. He was alleged of beating and quarrelling deceased under the influence of liquor and on the fateful night he picked up a log from the house and beaten deceased that caused internal injury in her stomach and murdered her. Appellant pleaded that death occurred due to cardiac arrest.

Hon'ble Apex Court Held, while dismissing the Appeal: It was the Appellant himself who took her to the hospital and made a false statement that she suffered a cardiac arrest but after the autopsy was conducted on the body of the deceased, it was opined that she died out of shock and haemorrhage due to thoracic injuries. In addition to other circumstances, the prosecution was able to establish that it was none other than the Appellant who had committed the crime and he wanted to show his innocence by taking the deceased to the hospital and made a false statement that she suffered a cardiac arrest which on receipt of the post-mortem certificate, was found to be false where it was established that the death was caused by homicidal violence.

The prosecution established chain of events that leave no matter of doubt that it is none other than the Appellant who had committed the crime of murdering his own wife.

The present case squarely rests on circumstantial evidence where the death has been caused by homicidal violence and the Appellant who had himself taken the deceased to the hospital and made a false statement to the Doctor that she had suffered a cardiac arrest which was found to be false after the postmortem report was received and the nature of injuries which were attributed on the body of the deceased of which a reference has been made clearly establish that it is the case where none other than the Accused Appellant has committed a commission of crime with intention to commit the murder of his own wife who was at the advanced stage of pregnancy. No substance in the appeal and is accordingly dismissed.

Appellant's bail bonds stand cancelled. The Appellant is directed to surrender within four weeks from today and undergo the remaining part of sentence.

Ratio Decidendi: Circumstances from which the conclusion of guilt is to be drawn should be fully proved and conclusive in nature.

SIXTEEN

UNION OF INDIA (UOI) AND ORS. VS. DHARAM PAL, 2019

Hon'ble Judges/Coram: N.V. Ramana, Mohan M. Shantanagoudar and S. Abdul Nazeer, JJ.

Citation: (2019)15SCC388, MANU/SC/0627/2019

Case Note: Criminal - Death penalty - Section 302/34 of Indian Penal Code, 1860 (IPC) and Section 30 of the Prisoners Act, 1894 - Instant appeal was directed by State against decision of High Court whereby the High Court allowed Writ Petition filed by Respondent Dharam Pal, and commuted death sentence awarded to him to life imprisonment - Respondent was tried and convicted under Section 302/34 of IPC for the commission of murder of five persons belonging to the same family - Whether High Court had erred in setting aside sentence of death of Respondent and commuting same into life imprisonment

Facts: Respondent Dharam Pal, in an earlier incident, was convicted under Section 376/452 of IPC vide judgment passed by the Additional Sessions Judge, and sentenced to undergo rigorous imprisonment for ten years. The Respondent was released on bail by the High Court while admitting his appeal, however on the intervening night, Respondent accompanied by his brother Nirmal Singh committed the murder of five persons who were the family members of the prosecutrix for whose rape the Respondent was convicted. The Respondent and his brother were tried and convicted under Section 302/34 of the IPC by the Sessions Court,. Vide its judgment, the said Court sentenced both the Accused to be hanged until death. Death Reference was heard and the conviction and sentence was affirmed by the High Court by its judgment. The Respondent and his brother, further filed an appeal before this Court, which came to be partly allowed, commuting the death sentence of the Respondent's brother Nirmal Singh into life imprisonment, but upheld the death sentence of the Respondent taking into account his conviction in the rape case, and commission of murder of five family members of the prosecutrix of that case while on bail. Respondent filed the impugned Writ Petition before the High Court praying for his death sentence to be commuted to life imprisonment in light of the change in circumstances viz. his acquittal in the rape case, which was an important deciding factor by this Court in negating his appeal. He also challenged it on grounds of delay in deciding his mercy petition by the President, among other grounds. The High Court while allowing his Writ Petition held that it is a case of violation of the fundamental rights of the Respondent, which makes him eligible for getting his death sentence commuted to life imprisonment, and orders were passed accordingly. The State has filed this appeal against the decision of the High Court.

Hon'ble Apex Court Held, while disposing of the appeal : 1. It is admitted that, the Respondent has undergone incarceration for a total period of over 25 years, out of which 18 years were in solitary confinement. Throughout the period of deciding his mercy petition by the President, he was kept in solitary confinement in various jails. Solitary confinement prior to the disposal of the mercy petition is per se illegal and amounts to separate and additional punishment not authorized by law. Section 30 of Act, 1894 provides that, every prisoner under sentence of death shall, immediately on his arrival in the prison after sentence, be searched by, or by order of, the Jailer and all articles shall be taken from him which the Jailer deems it dangerous or inexpedient to leave in his possession. Every such prisoner shall be confined in a cell apart from all other prisoners, and shall be placed by day and by night under the charge of a guard.

2. Thus, solitary confinement prior to the rejection of mercy petition, which has taken place in spite of various decisions of this Court to the contrary, is unfortunate and palpably illegal. In the present case, the Respondent underwent such a long period of solitary confinement that too, prior to his mercy petition being rejected, thereby making it a formidable case for commuting his death sentence into life imprisonment, as rightly

held by the High Court.

3. High Court examined the inordinate delay in disposing the mercy petition in the right perspective to hold it illegal, and thereafter commuted the sentence to life imprisonment in light of principles of law laid down in Shatrughan Chauhan. These aspects, coupled with the fact that the authorities did not place the records regarding the acquittal of the Respondent in the rape case before the President for consideration of the mercy petition has caused grave injustice and prejudice against the Respondent. On receipt of a mercy petition, the Department concerned has to call for all the records and materials connected with the conviction. When the matter is placed before the President, it is incumbent on the part of the concerned authority to place all the materials such as judgments of the courts, as well as any other relevant material connected with the conviction. In the present case, this Court while upholding the death sentence of the Respondent and commuting the sentence of his brother to life imprisonment had placed reliance on the fact that the Respondent was convicted in the rape case, and the persons who he had killed were the family members of the prosecutrix of the rape case. The fact that he was subsequently acquitted for that case has great bearing on the quantum on sentence that ought to be awarded to the Respondent and the same should have been brought to the notice of the President while deciding his mercy petition. Failure to do so has caused irreparable prejudice against the Respondent.

4. High Court has not erred in setting aside the sentence of death of the Respondent and commuting the same into life imprisonment. In view of reasons discussed and unconscionable delay of more than 13 years in deciding the mercy petition, the failure to produce the relevant documents regarding the Respondent before the President for deciding the mercy petition, and that the Respondent has undergone 18 years of illegal solitary confinement, there is no reason to interfere with the decision of the High Court. However, considering the fact that the Respondent had violated the conditions of bail imposed on him by the High Court in criminal appeal, as he had committed the murder of five persons while on bail, cannot be overlooked while quantifying the actual sentence. It would be appropriate to direct the release of the Respondent after the completion of 35 years of actual imprisonment including the period already undergone by him.

5. Appeal disposed off.

SEVENTEEN

Manoj Kumar Khokhar Vs. State of Rajasthan and Ors., 2022

Hon'ble Judges/Coram: M.R. Shah and B.V. Nagarathna, JJ.

Act/ Sections: Code of Criminal Procedure, 1973 (CrPC) - Section 437, Code of Criminal Procedure, 1973 (CrPC) - Section 437(3), Code of Criminal Procedure, 1973 (CrPC) - Section 439, Code of Criminal Procedure, 1973 (CrPC) - Section 439(2); Constitution of India - Article 21; Indian Penal Code, 1860 (IPC) - Section 120B, Indian Penal Code, 1860 (IPC) - Section 148, Indian Penal Code, 1860 (IPC) - Section 149, Indian Penal Code, 1860 (IPC) - Section 300, Indian Penal Code, 1860 (IPC) - Section 302

No. of pages of the Original Judgement: 11

Citation: AIR2022SC364, (2022)3SCC501, MANU/SC/0028/2022

Case Note: Criminal - Bail - Appeal against grant thereof - FIR alleged commission of offence under Section 302 of the Indian Penal Code, 1860 (IPC) - Pre-existing rivalry between Accused, his brothers and deceased - Accused enlarged on Bail - Hence the present appeal - Whether bail granted liable to be set aside?

Facts: Appellant is the son of deceased and one who lodged the First Information Report for alleged offence under Section 302 IPC against R2/ Accused. As alleged in the FIR lodged by Appellant, he was attacked by the Respondent-Accused with the intention of killing him. Respondent-Accused pinned the deceased to the ground, sat on his chest and forcefully strangled him, thereby causing his death. As stated in the FIR, there was a pre-existing rivalry between the Respondent-Accused, his brothers and the deceased. The Respondent-Accused was arrested and remained under judicial custody for nearly one year and five months till granted bail by the High Court vide impugned order.

Hon'ble Apex Court Held, while allowing the Appeal: Court considering an application for bail has to exercise discretion in a judicious manner and in accordance with the settled principles of law having regard to the crime alleged to be committed by the Accused on the one hand and ensuring purity of the trial of the case on the other.

While elaborate reasons may not be assigned for grant of bail or an extensive discussion of the merits of the case may not be undertaken by the court considering a bail application, an order de hors reasoning or bereft of the relevant reasons cannot result in grant of bail.

Having considered facts of the present case, case not considered fit for grant of bail to the Respondent-Accused, having regard to the seriousness of the allegations against him.

High Court has lost sight of the aforesaid material aspects of the case and has, by a very cryptic and casual order, de hors coherent reasoning, granted bail to the Accused. Hence the impugned order set aside. The appeal is allowed.

PPP

EIGHTEEN

Kamla Devi Vs. State of Rajasthan and Ors., 2022

Hon'ble Judges/Coram: M.R. Shah and B.V. Nagarathna, JJ.

Act/ Sections: Code of Criminal Procedure, 1973 (CrPC) - Section 107, Code of Criminal Procedure, 1973 (CrPC) - Section 116(3), Code of Criminal Procedure, 1973 (CrPC) - Section 439, Code of Criminal Procedure, 1973 (CrPC) - Section 439(2); Constitution of India - Article 136; Indian Penal Code, 1860 (IPC) - Section 34, Indian Penal Code, 1860 (IPC) - Section 201, Indian Penal Code, 1860 (IPC) - Section 302

No. of pages of the Original Judgement: 08

Citation: AIR2022SC1524, MANU/SC/0312/2022

Case Note: Criminal - Grant of bail - Validity - Section 302, 201 and 34 of the Indian Penal Code, 1860 (IPC) - Present appeals have been preferred by the Appellant who is the wife of the deceased, challenging orders passed by the High Court, whereby bail has been granted to the two Accused - Whether impugned order of bail is liable to be set aside?

Facts: The Respondents-Accused preferred separate bail applications before the High Court and by the impugned orders, the High Court has enlarged them on bail in the case arising out of FIR. Being aggrieved by the grant of bail to the Respondents-Accused, the Appellant-wife of the deceased has preferred the instant appeals before this Court. The Appellant submitted that the High Court has not properly exercised its discretionary power to grant bail to the Respondents-Accused in a judicious manner. The High

Court, in the impugned orders, had failed to consider the severity of the offences alleged against the Respondents-Accused and the brutal manner in which the offences were committed and attempted to be concealed by throwing the body of the deceased, together with the murder weapon, into a well.

Hon'ble Apex Court Held, while allowing the appeal: 1. This Court has, on several occasions has discussed the factors to be considered by a Court while deciding a bail application. The primary considerations which must be placed at balance while deciding the grant of bail are: (i) the seriousness of the offence; (ii) the likelihood of the Accused fleeing from justice; (iii) the impact of release of the Accused on the prosecution witnesses; (iv) likelihood of the Accused tampering with evidence. While such list is not exhaustive, it may be stated that if a Court takes into account such factors in deciding a bail application, it could be concluded that the decision has resulted from a judicious exercise of its discretion.

2. It is not necessary for a Court to give elaborate reasons while granting bail, particularly when the case is at the initial stage and the allegations of the offences by the Accused would not have been crystalised as such. There cannot be elaborate details recorded to give an impression that the case is one that would result in a conviction or, by contrast, in an acquittal while passing an order on an application for grant of bail. However, the Court deciding a bail application cannot completely divorce its decision from material aspects of the case such as the allegations made against the Accused; severity of the punishment if the allegations are proved beyond reasonable doubt which would result in a conviction; reasonable apprehension of the witnesses being influenced by the Accused; tampering of the evidence; the frivolity in the case of the prosecution; criminal antecedents of the Accused; and a prima-facie satisfaction of the Court in support of the charge against the Accused.

3. The allegations against the Respondents-Accused are under Section 302, 201 and 34 of the Indian Penal Code, with regard to the murder of Sohan Singh, husband of the Appellant herein. The offences alleged against the Respondents-Accused are of grave nature. The accusation against the Accused is that they committed the offence of murder on the deceased and attempted to clandestinely dispose off the dead body of the deceased and the lathis used to attack him, by throwing the same in a well nearby so as to conceal the offence. It is also the case of the Appellant that following the

release of Accused-Kishan Singh on bail, he had threatened the Appellant herein with dire consequences for pursuing the criminal trial. A complaint in this regard also came to be filed against Kishan Singh. Thus, the possibility of the Accused threatening or otherwise influencing the witnesses, if on bail, cannot be ruled out.

4. Present case is not a fit case for the grant of bail to the Respondents-Accused, given the seriousness of the allegations against them.

5. The High Court has granted bail to the Respondents-Accused by passing a very cryptic and casual order, de hors cogent reasoning. The High Court was not right in allowing the applications for bail filed by the Respondents Accused. Hence the impugned orders are set aside. The appeals are allowed.

6. The Respondents-Accused are on bail. Their bail bonds stand cancelled and they are directed to surrender before the concerned jail authorities within a period of two weeks.

NINETEEN

DINUBHAI BOGHABHAI SOLANKI VS. STATE OF GUJARAT AND ORS., 2017

Hon'ble Judges/Coram: A.K. Sikri and Ashok Bhushan, JJ.

Act/ Sections: INDIAN PENAL CODE, 1860 (IPC) - Section 114; INDIAN PENAL CODE, 1860 (IPC) - Section 302; ARMS ACT 1959 - Section 25(1)

No. of pages of the Original Judgement: 19

Citation: AIR2017SC5690, (2018)11SCC129, MANU/SC/1365/2017

Case Note: Criminal - De novo retrial - Validity thereof - Sections 302 and 114 of Indian Penal Code, 1860 (IPC); Section 25(1) of Arms Act, 1959 - Present appeal filed challenging order whereby High Court directed de novo trial of case - Whether High Court justified passing de novo trial of case

Facts: An activist, who made a complaint against illegal mining, was murdered. An FIR was registered. The Appellant was an accused in offence of murder. Investigation was lackadaisical. The complainant was forced to approach High Court to seek necessary directions for proper investigation. The High Court directed de novo trial of case with specific directions. Aggrieved by present appeal was filed.

Hon'ble Apex Court Held, while disposing of appeal: (i) There was no suggestion that the Appellant and his nephew were persons responsible for murder of activist. That charge which was levelled against them and other Accused persons had to be proved in the trial by cogent evidence.

Standard of proof that was required in such criminal cases was that, guilt had to be proved beyond reasonable doubt. However, at same time, it was also necessary to ensure that, trial was conducted fairly where witnesses were able to depose truthfully and fearlessly. Guilt of an Accused was to be proved beyond reasonable doubt. Even in a case of a slight doubt about guilt of under trial, he was entitled to benefit of doubt. All these principles were premised on doctrine that, "ten criminals might go unpunished but one innocent person should not be convicted". Emphasis here was on ensuring that; innocent person should not be convicted. Convicting an innocence leads to serious flaws in the criminal justice system.

(ii) In view of exceptional circumstances in which retrial was ordered by the High Court, and was being maintained in principle, with only modification that instead of all witnesses, 26 witnesses would be re-examined, Supreme Court opined that, in order to ensure that, there was a fair trial in literal sense of term, at least till the time eight eye-witnesses were re-examined, the Appellant should remain in confinement and he be released thereafter with certain conditions, pending remaining trial. Bails granted to the Appellant by present Court was cancelled for the time being.

ÞÞÞ

TWENTY

KRISHNAKANT TAMRAKAR VS. THE STATE OF MADHYA PRADESH, 2018

Hon'ble Judges/Coram: Adarsh Kumar Goel and U.U. Lalit, JJ.

Act/ Sections: Commercial Courts Act, 2015; Arbitration and Conciliation Act, 1996; Advocate Act, 1961; Negotiable Instruments Act, 1881; Right to Information Act, 2005; Indian Penal Code, 1860 (IPC) - Section 148, Indian Penal Code, 1860 (IPC) - Section 302, Indian Penal Code, 1860 (IPC) - Section 149; Code of Criminal Procedure, 1973 (CrPC) - Section 167, Code of Criminal Procedure, 1973 (CrPC) - Section 436A; Constitution of India - Article 14, Constitution of India - Article 21, Constitution of India - Article 143(1), Constitution of India - Article 226, Constitution of India - Article 227

No. of pages of the Original Judgement: 17

Citation: AIR2018SC3635, MANU/SC/0310/2018

Case Note: Criminal - Bail application - Pendency thereof - Sections 148, 149 and 302 of Indian Penal Code, 1860 - Appellant applied for bail pending consideration of appeal before High Court - High Court rejected bail application with observation that evidence on record did not warrant grant of bail - Order of High Court was challenged on ground that Appellant had been in custody for more than ten years and remedy of appeal would be meaningless if he had to remain in custody for full term of sentence - Hence, present appeal by Appellant - Whether having regard to nature of jurisdiction of High Court and present volume of work, expectation for speedy disposal of criminal appeals was realistic or there was need for re-engineering of judicial structure

Facts: Appellant was convicted under Sections 148 and 302 read with 149 of Code by Trial Court. Appellant applied for bail pending consideration of appeal before High Court. After said prayer was rejected, another application was filed. High Court rejected second bail application with observation that evidence on record did not warrant grant of bail. Order of High Court was challenged on ground that Appellant had been in custody for more than ten years and remedy of appeal would be meaningless if he had to remain in custody for full term of sentence. Hence, present appeal by Appellant.

Hon'ble Apex Court Held, while disposing off the appeal: (i) Ministry was directed to present at least quarterly report on strikes/abstaining from work, loss caused and action proposed. Matter could be considered in its contempt or inherent jurisdiction of Court. The Court may hold that office bearers of Bar Association/Bar Council who passed resolution for strike or abstaining from work, were liable to be restrained from appearing before any Court for specified period or until such time as they purge themselves of contempt to satisfaction of Chief Justice of concerned High Court based on appropriate undertaking/conditions. They might also be liable to be removed from position of office bearers of Bar Association forthwith until Chief Justice of concerned High Court so permits on appropriate undertaking being filed by them. Matter might also be considered by Present Court on receipt of report from High Courts in this regard. That did not debar report/petition from any other source even before end of quarter, if situation so warrants.

(ii) Based on Law Commission Report, concerned authorities might examine whether there was need for any changes in judicial structure by creating appropriate fora to decongest Constitutional Courts so as to realistically achieve constitutional goal of speedy justice. There was need to consider whether there should be body of full time experts without affecting independence of judiciary, to assist in identifying, scrutinizing and evaluating candidates at pre-appointment stage and to evaluate performance post appointment.

❦❦❦

TWENTY-ONE

Barun Chandra Thakur Vs. Central Bureau of Investigation and Ors., 2017

Hon'ble Judges/Coram: R.K. Agrawal and Abhay Manohar Sapre, JJ.

Act/ Sections: Indian Penal Code, 1860 (IPC) - Section 34; Indian Penal Code, 1860 (IPC) - Section 302; ARMS ACT 1959 - Section 25; Juvenile Justice (Care and Protection of Children) Act, 2000 [Repealed] - Section 75; PROTECTION OF CHILDREN FROM SEXUAL OFFENCES ACT, 2012 - Section 12

No. of pages of the Original Judgement: 07

Citation: AIR2017SC5735, (2018)12SCC119, MANU/SC/1576/2017

Case Note: Criminal - Grant of interim bail - Maintainability thereof - Sections 34 and 302 of Indian Penal Code, 1860 - Section 25 of Arms Act, 1959 - Section 75 of Juvenile Justice Act, 2000 - Section 12 of Protection of Children from Sexual Offences Act, 2012 - Petition was filed by Respondent for grant of interim bail - High Court granted interim bail for offences punishable under Sections of different Acts - Present appeal filed against order of High Court whereby High Court had granted interim bail to Respondents till presentation of challan subject to certain conditions - Whether order granting interim bail to Respondents was maintainable

Facts: Petition was filed by Respondent for grant of interim bail. High Court granted interim bail for the offences punishable under Sections 302 read with Section 34 of Code, Section 25 of Arms Act, Section 75 of the JJ Act and Section 12 of POCSO, Act, 2012 till next date on their furnishing bonds to the satisfaction of Investigation Agency. Appellants filed special leave petition to High Court which was disposed off making absolute the interim bail granted to Respondents till presentation of the challan subject to certain conditions. Hence, present appeal was filed by Appellants.

Hon'ble Apex Court Held, while dismissing the appeal: (i) Respondents could not be held guilty of any suppression, concealment or fraud for the simple reason that the petitions were prepared and accepted by the Registry of High Court. The fact relating to the withdrawal of the Resolution passed by the District Bar Associations could not be said to be in the knowledge of Respondents.

(ii) CBI was yet to examine and analyse the role of the Respondents and there was no evidence of their complicity in the crime and there was not even a pointer of involvement of Respondents in the alleged crime. Their involvement could no be established until and unless, there was some substantial evidence against them. High Court while granting interim bail to Respondents till the presentation of Challan had laid down conditions that Respondents should make themselves available for interrogation by the investigating agency as and when required and Respondents should not, directly or indirectly, make any inducement, threat or promise to any person acquainted with the facts of the accusation against them so as to dissuade him from disclosing such facts to the Court or to investigating agency. Respondents should not leave country without the prior permission of the Court.

(iii) Order passed by High Court granting interim bail to the answering Respondents till the presentation of Challan could not be faulted with.

Adv. Jayprakash Somani's Videos On Law

1) SLP in Supreme Court / Special Leave Petitions in the Supreme Court of India

2) Transfer of Civil & Criminal Cases by the Supreme Court of India / Transfer of Matrimonial Cases

3) Appellate Jurisdiction of the Supreme Court of India

4) Jurisdictions of the Supreme Court of India

5) Public Interest Litigation in the Supreme Court of India / PIL in Supreme Court

6) Article 32 Writ Petitions in the Supreme Court of India

7) Bail Matters Top 10 Supreme Court Cases

8) FIR Quashing in High Court & Supreme Court

9) Bail & Anticipatory Bail Matters in Supreme Court

10) Insolvency & Bankruptcy Matters in the Supreme Court

11) Insolvency & Bankruptcy Code 2016 Part 1

12) Insolvency & Bankruptcy Code 2016 Part 2

13) Insolvency & Bankruptcy Code 2016 Part 3

14) Corporate Liquidation Process

15) Supreme Court Rules & Procedures Webinar of 2.5 hour on Zoom

16) RDDBFI Act, 1993 (Introduction)

17) The Indian Contact Act 1872

18) Negotiable Instruments Act (Introduction)

19) How to avoid matrimonial disputes& some more videos

20) SEBI Matters in the Supreme Court

21) Matrimonial Matters: Supreme Court's 20 Case Laws

22) Consumer Matters Supreme Court's 20 Case Laws

23) Service Matters Supreme Court's 20 Case Laws

24) How to Search Lawyer for Your Matter

25) Property Matters Supreme Court's 20 Case Laws

26) Bail Matters: Supreme Court's 20 Case Laws

27) Supreme Court / High Court Vacation Benches

28) 69000 Teacher's Recruitment Matters of UP Government in the Supreme Court

29) Contempt of Court Matters in the Supreme Court

30) Advocate Act's Matters in the Supreme Court

31) Business Law Matters in the Supreme Court

32) Banking Matters in the Supreme Court

33) Labour Law Matters in the Supreme Court

34) Arbitration Matters in the Supreme Court

35) Careers in Law -Zoom Webinar by Adv. Jayprakash Somani

36) Civil Matters in the Supreme Court

37) Consumer Protection Act | Consumer Matters in the Supreme Court

38) Corporate Matters in the Supreme Court

39) Criminal Matters in the Supreme Court

40) Role of Respondent in the Supreme Court of India

41) Motor Vehicle Accident Matters in Supreme Court with case laws

42) Article 131 Original Suits in Supreme Court

43) PIL in Supreme Court/ Public Interest Litigations in the Supreme Court of India'

44) CAB Citizenship Amendment Bill is not Unconstitutional

45) Supreme Court of India Cases & Process – Marathi

46) Legal Services Export / Export of Legal Services

47) Transfer of Matrimonial Cases by the Supreme Court of India

48) Public Interest Litigation PIL

49) The Specific Relief Act (Introduction)

50) Corporate Insolvency Resolution Process CIRP

51) ABMM's Career 5 - Careers in Law

52) Transfer of cases by Supreme Court

53) Writ Petitions in High Court & Supreme Court of India

54) Supreme Court Jurisdictions - Appeals, SLP, Writ Petitions, Transfer, Original, Review, Curative

55) LEGAL INDIA TV Show: Cases Handled in Supreme Court

56) Corporate Liquidation Process

57) Legal Services Export / Export of Legal Services

58) Corporate Laws

59) Election Matters- Supreme Court's 20 Case Laws

60) Companies Act, 2013

62) Competition Act, 2002

63) Banking Matters - Supreme Court's 20 Case Laws

64) Election Matters in the Supreme Court

65) Armed Forces Tribunal Matters in the Supreme Court

66) Compassionate Appointment Service matter

67) Foreign Exchange Management Act FEMA

68) Foreign Trade Policy 2021-26 Proposed

69) Customs Act 1962

70) Narcotic Drugs and Psychotropic Substances Act, 1985 NDPS Act

71) Foreign Trade Development & Regulation Act, 1992

72) How to Search Good Advocate in the Supreme Court of India

73) Sr. Adv Vikas Singh's Interview in Nani Palkhivala Wednesday Law Club

74) Indian Penal Code (I. P. C.)

75) Criminal Procedure Code (Cr. P. C.)

76) Commercial Courts & International Arbitration - by Mr. Jaideep Gupta, Senior Advocate in Nani Palkhivala Wednesday Law Club

77) Sr. Adv Ranji Thomos in Nani Palkhivala Wednesday Law Club

78) Urgent Matters in Supreme Court during vacations

79) 498A Bail Matters in Supreme Court

81) 376 Bail Matters in Supreme Court

82) 302, 304, 307, 308 Bail Matters in Supreme Court

83) 138, 420 Bail Matters in Supreme Court

84) POCSO Act Bail Matters in Supreme Court

85) NDPS Act Bail Matters in Supreme Court

86) What is ED (Enforcement Directorate)?

87) Prevention of Money Laundering Act, 2002 (PMLA Act)

88) Insolvency & Bankruptcy Code- Supreme Court Case Laws. Webinar in Nani Palkhivala Wednesday Law Club

89) What is NCLT & NCLAT?

90) Acquittal from 376- Supreme Court's some case laws in Nani Palkhivala Wednesday Law Club dt 28.7.22

91) Insolvency & Bankruptcy in India

92) Can we file case directly in the Supreme Court?

93) Adv. Anuja Pethia has cleared AOR Exam 2021 with 77% marks - Her interview in Nani Palkhivala Wednesday Law Club

94) Customs Act - Supreme Court Case Laws & Interview of AOR Adv. Anuja Pethia in Nani Palkhivala Law Club.

95) The Uttar Pradesh Public Service Tribunals Act, 1976

96) POCSO Act - Supreme Court Case Laws & Interview of AOR Adv. Shoumendu Mukharji & Adv. Nishant Verma in Nani Palkhivala Law Club.

97) Who Can Trigger CIRP Process Under Insolvency Law of India

98) The Uttar Pradesh Government Servant Discipline and Appeal Rules, 1999

99) CIRP Application Under Sec 7 by FC

100) Information Technology Act 2000

101) Uttar Pradesh Recruitment of Dependants of Government Servants Dying in Harness Rules, 1974

102) Foreign Exchange Management Act 1999 & Supreme Court's Case Laws on FEMA & Leading Case of AOR Exam in Nani Palkhivala Law Club.

103) Arbitration and Conciliation Act 1996 & It's Supreme Court Case Laws in Nani Palkhivala Wednesday Law Club.

104) Narcotic Drugs & Psychotropic Substances Act 1985 (NDPS Act) & It's Supreme Court Case Laws in Nani Palkhivala Wednesday Law Club.

105) Recovery of Debts and Bankruptcy Act 1993

106) Uttar Pradesh Land Revenue Code 2006

107) CIRP Application Under Sec 9 by OC

108) CIRP Application Under Sec 10 by CD

109) Hindu Succession Act, 1956

110) Maharashtra Civil Services Rules, 1981

111) Indian Contract Act, 1872 & Supreme Court's Case Laws" in Nani Palkhiwala Wednesday Law Club

112) Securities and Exchange Board of India Act, 1992 i. e. SEBI Act 1992 & Case Laws on Insiders Trading" in Nani Palkhiwala Wednesday Law Club

113) Moratorium Under Section 14 of IBC, 2016

114) Hindu Marriage Act, 1955

115) Maharashtra Land Revenue Code, 1966

116) 64 Leading Cases of AOR Exam Session 1 :- Cases 1 to16 in Nani Palkhiwala Wednesday Law Club

117) 64 Leading Cases of AOR Exam Session 2: Cases 17 to 32 in Nani Palkhivala Wednesday Law Club

118) 64 Leading Cases of AOR Examination Session 3: Cases 33 to 48 in Nani Palkhivala Wednesday Law Club

119) 64 Leading Cases of AOR Exam Session 4: Cases 49 to 64 in Nani Palkhivala Wednesday Law Club

List Of Adv. Jayprakash Somani's Published Books

1. Supreme Court of India's Leading Case Laws on 'Insolvency & Bankruptcy Code 2016'
2. Bail Matters – Supreme Court's Latest Leading Case Laws
3. Arbitration Matters- Supreme Court's Latest Leading Case Laws
4. Property Matters - Supreme Court's Latest Leading Case Laws
5. Matrimonial Matters- Supreme Court's Latest Leading Case Laws
6. Election Matters- Supreme Court's Latest Leading Case Laws
7. SEBI Matters- Supreme Court's Latest Leading Case Laws
8. Banking Matters- Supreme Court's Latest Leading Case Laws
9. Service Matters- Supreme Court's Latest Leading Case Laws
10. Contempt of Court Matters- Supreme Court's Latest Leading Case Laws
11. Consumer Protection Matters- Supreme Court's Latest Leading Case Laws
12. Corporate Law- Supreme Court's Latest Leading Case Laws
13. Supreme Court's AOR Exam- Leading Cases
14. Armed Force Tribunal - Supreme Court's Latest Leading Case Laws
15. Acquittal From 376 - Supreme Court's Latest Leading Case Laws
16. Negotiable instrument – Supreme Court's Latest Leading Case Laws
17. Contract Act- Supreme Court's Latest Leading Case Laws
18. Insider trading- Supreme Court's Latest Leading Case Laws
19. Foreign Exchange and Management Act- Supreme Court's Latest Leading Case Laws
20. Income Tax Act- Supreme Court's Latest Leading Case Laws
21. Company Law- Supreme Court's Latest Leading Case Laws
22. Competition & Monopoly Matters- Supreme Court's Latest Leading Case Laws
23. Compassionate Appointment- Service Matters- Supreme Court's Latest Leading Case Laws
24. Compulsory Retirement- Service Matters- Supreme Court's Latest Leading Case Laws
25. Voluntary Retirement- Service Matters- Supreme Court's Latest Leading Case Laws
26. Removal/Dismissal/Termination from Service- Supreme Court's Latest Leading Case Laws

27. Seniority- Service Matter- Supreme Court's Latest Leading Case Laws

28. Promotion- Service Matter- Supreme Court's Latest Leading Case Laws

29. Equal Pay for Equal Work- Service Matter- Supreme Court's Latest Leading Case Laws

30. Condition of Service- Service Matter- Supreme Court's Latest Leading Case Laws

31. Customs Act- Supreme Court's Leading Case Laws

32. Information Technology Act- Supreme Court's Leading Case Laws

33. SEC. 125 CR. P. C.- Supreme Court's Leading Case Laws

34. SEC. 498A OF I. P. C.- Supreme Court's Leading Case Laws

35. MOTOR VEHICLE ACT- Supreme Court's Leading Case Laws

36. CONDITION OF SERVICE- SERVICE MATTER- Supreme Court's Leading Case Laws

37. SUSPENSION- SERVICE MATTER- Supreme Court's Leading Case Laws

38. Reservation in SC, ST, OBC- Service Matter- Supreme Court's Leading Case Laws

39. NARCOTIC DRUGS AND PSYCHOTROPIC SUBSTANCES (NDPS) ACT - Supreme Court of India's Latest Leading Case Laws

40. SEC 302 IPC - Supreme Court of India's Latest Leading Case Laws

41. PROTECTION OF CHILDREN FROM SEXUAL OFFENCES ACT (POCSO) - Supreme Court of India's Latest Leading Case Laws

42. PMLA ACT BAIL MATTERS - Supreme Court of India's Leading Case Laws

43. SEC 376 BAIL MATTERS - Supreme Court of India's Leading Case Laws

44. SEC 302 BAIL MATTERS - Supreme Court of India's Leading Case Laws

45. POCSO ACT BAIL MATTERS - Supreme Court of India's Leading Case Laws

46 . JUVENILE JUSTICE ACT- Supreme Court of India's Leading Case Laws

47. TRANSFER OF PROPERTY ACT- Supreme Court of India's Leading Case Laws

48. PROFESSIONAL ETHICS OF ADVOCATES- AOR EXAM- SUPREME COURT'S LEADING CASE LAWS

49. TRANSFER OF PROPERTY ACT- Supreme Court of India's Leading Case Laws

Books are available online in India

1. Notion Press: https://notionpress.com/author/jayprakash_somani

2. Amazon: https://www.amazon.in/s?k=jayprakash+somani

3. Flipkart: https://www.flipkart.com/search?q=Jayprakash%20Somani

Books are available online at International Market

4. Amazon International: https://www.amazon.com/s?k=jayprakash+somani

5. Amazon United Kingdom: https://www.amazon.co.uk/s?k=jayprakash+somani

6. E-Books/Kindle edition at National & International Level: https://www.amazon.in/s?k=jaypraksh+somani

9 798890 660510

Printed by Libri Plureos GmbH in Hamburg,
Germany